Collecting
Carnival Glass

Marion Quintin-Baxendale

Francis Joseph
1998

Dedication

In memory of my dear father, recently passed away, and my late good friends Julie and Liliane.
And with thanks to all my family and many friends who encouraged me in the researching and writing
of this book, especially Gunnar Lersjo, glass historian and principal photographer.
Without each and every one of you, this book would not have been written.

Introduction

This book is intended to serve primarily as a Pattern-name identification book for collectors of
'Carnival Glass' (ie iridised pressed glassware) worldwide, and also offers a Price Guide for the
patterns depicted.

The author has collected Carnival Glass for over thirty years and has researched extensively
at Factory sources throughout America, Australia, Northern Europe and Scandinavia.

Previously unpublished research material is included in this book, reflecting the ever-growing
interest of Carnival Glass collectors worldwide. Awareness of the production history of this
internationally produced glassware continues to grow apace.

The author hopes this book will contribute more knowledge to this particular field and at the
same time bring much pleasure to its readers.

© M. Quintin-Baxendale under licence to Francis Joseph 1988

Published in the UK by
Francis Joseph Publications
5 Southbrook Mews, London SE12 8LG

Production	Francis Salmon
Scanning	Gabriel Granger
Typesetting	John Folkard E J Folkard Computer Services 199 Station Road, Crayford, Kent DA1 3QF
Printing	Greenwich Press Ltd Eastmoor Street, London SE7

ISBN 1-870703-71-5

Contents

Chapter One:

The Origins of Carnival Glass worldwide

Here is a list of the ten major questions that collectors ask themselves when they first decide to collect Carnival Glass: (1) What exactly *is* Carnival Glass? (2) What is *reproduction* Carnival Glass? (3) What is *new* Carnival Glass? (4) What brought about the production of Carnival Glass? (5) Which shapes were produced in Carnival Glass? (6) Which base-glass colours were used in production? (7) What is the *iridisation overlay* on Carnival Glass? (8) Where was Carnival Glass sold and why? (9) What sort of patterning, if any, appears on this ware? and (10) Why is this type of glassware called Carnival Glass?

And now come the answers to these questions!

WHAT EXACTLY *IS* CARNIVAL GLASS?

It is, quite simply, **iridised press-moulded glassware**. It is **not** iridised blown glass, so it has **mould lines**, even though these can be heavily disguised by the intricate patterning that nearly always accompanies this ware. Although usually press-moulded, some blow-moulded pieces are also accepted by collectors as an extension of the Carnival Glass tradition. The earliest production (from c1905-1930s worldwide) is much sought after by collectors, either individually or through Carnival Glass Collectors Clubs, or private antique shops or auction purchases.

Carnival Glassware was first produced in commercial quantities in America, followed by England and Australia and later by Glass Houses in the Scandinavian and Baltic areas and in Czechoslovakia. There was limited and prior experimental production in Czechoslovakia and in France and Belgium, but the opportunity to market was not followed up, except in old Czechoslovakia, and then not until *after* the established success of the American and other producer areas.

This highly pattern-detailed and colourful domestic glassware glass was an inexpensive substitute for the more costly iridised art glass. It eventually fell from popularity as the Art Deco period dawned. This brought about artistic changes which influenced the buying public, so that this highly ornate iridised pressed ware fell out of fashion. Market forces also changed and deteriorated with the Great Depression. Thus by the mid 1930's only the later Scandinavian factories were still out-putting their own particular Carnival Glass. Here it was known as Pressed Lustre Ware.

WHAT IS *REPRODUCTION* CARNIVAL GLASS?

Over forty years after the demise of sales and production of the first Carnival Glass, there was an unexpected revival in the early 1960s in America.

Imperial began reproducing Carnival Glass using some of the original moulds. This glass was marked with an "IG" on the base. A few original moulds from the earlier production lines were also acquired by various individuals or Companies and used to reproduce other of the earlier ware. Unfortunately these pieces were often placed on the market without even identifying the product as new. Carnival Glass from this era is now also collectable (it had a short life-span!) and is generally referred to as Reproduction Carnival Glass. Imperial eventually closed down for good in 1982.

WHAT IS NEW CARNIVAL GLASS?

There is a continuing and growing market for pieces produced far later than the original ware, (that is, as produced in modern times, but adhering closely to the traditional type of Carnival Glass). This latter production is of interest to lovers of Carnival Glass in its own right as it continues the manufacturing traditions of the past but uses new patterns and new colours and new techniques as well as those carried over from the earliest production period.

This is called New Carnival Glass.

Fenton Art Glass USA (a prime early producer) carries on this tradition as one of the present day Major manufacturers. Its glass is clearly marked with the Company name on the base of each piece and this is marketed as NEW CARNIVAL.

FAKE CARNIVAL GLASS

Unfortunately for collectors of both old and new Carnival Glass there is yet another market emerging from Taiwan where iridised pressed glassware is produced and marketed abroad. Pieces are marketed *faking* the old American Carnival Glass.

Patterns such as the American Peacocks on the Fence have been seen stacked a dozen or so high in one of the largest UK Antiques Markets – and herein lies the rub – the prices are as high as for the earlier genuine article – so watch out!

To make matters worse, some pieces have a fake Northwood 'N' mark on the base!. Other pieces seen in UK are taken from the earlier Dugan, Fenton and Cambridge patterns – Grape and Cable, and Cherry and Cable being quite common. These pieces are all of *much heavier* and *thicker base glass* than the genuine article, with a rather overwhelming iridescence -"too good to be true", as the saying goes. The best guide to these fakes is that they *look too new* . So far only American pattern pieces are known to have been copied, though there are also other designs selling that do not follow the established early Carnival Glass patterns.

WHAT BROUGHT ABOUT THE PRODUCTION OF CARNIVAL GLASS?

Now why did this particular type of glassware come into being? What were the market forces that generated such an interesting and long-lasting production?

In the early 1900s, iridised blown glassware was already available, following the Art nouveau design traditions, but this was quite expensive. Blow moulded and press-moulded iridised glassware could be produced much more inexpensively and so the Glasshouses attempted to develop a market for such ware. Pressed non iridised ware was already familiar to the public.

Thus the concept of Carnival Glass (as it was later named) came into being. It bridged a gap in the market- providing a colourful alternative to the more usual pressed glassware, and it was less costly than the other options mentioned, so ideal for a mass market production. In an age when the average home was still not brilliantly lit, the coloured lustre glow of the Carnival Glass was a sure-fire winner for the buying public.

It looked attractive and interesting, and it opened up the possibility of owning such ware quite inexpensively. This ware had, in effect, the essential "popular appeal of the moment". The various glass factories had found a new niche in their markets!

WHICH SHAPES WERE PRODUCED IN CARNIVAL GLASS AND WHY?

The reader will find a list of the majority of shapes produced in Chapter Two of this book.

It suffices here simply to state that the glass was developed specifically for use on the domestic market. So it was was first made into simple bowls and vases, using designs that included flora and fauna patterns as well as geometric shapes. All of these had intricate patterning which cleverly disguised any mould join lines.

Faults encountered either in the glass production technique or in using less costly raw materials for manufacture were well disguised by such complexities of colour and design. This permitted a considerable reduction in production costs, and offered a good value-for-money approach to the buying public.

There were many skilled glassworkers on hand as well as the experienced mould workers needed to produce the intricate mould work required. It was after all, prior to the Great Depression era, and the glasshouses in America and elsewhere already produced vast quantities of pressed glassware, in non-iridised form, as well as iridised blown glassware.

Production soon expanded since the required knowledge in using iridescence on coloured glass was already on hand from the Iridised Art Glass market (such as Steuben, with his 'Aurene' and Tiffany with his 'Favrile' and the production of such as Loetz and Daum ware.)

The public was eager to obtain domestic glassware now it was offered at such a competitive price and with such a new and colourful presentation.

The range of Carnival Glass on offer was expanded by the addition of water sets, table sets, punch bowls, perfume and dressing table sets, liqueur bottles, lamps, paperweights, hatpin holders, – a myriad of possibilities were explored and taken up! Even Souvenir and Commemorative pieces were produced.

WHICH BASE GLASS COLOURS WERE USED?
There were many colours used and these are detailed in Chapter Three of this book. But as a general comment it can be noted that each producer vied strenuously with his competitors to try and secure a leader-role footing in this market. So as many variations in colour as were technically possible to produce at market- viable prices were introduced.

WHAT IS MEANT BY 'IRIDISATION' UPON THE GLASS?
The iridescence was applied to the glass as it came from the press-mould either by re-firing, or later, by the less expensive method of spraying. The iridescence is ESSENTIAL to Carnival Glass. The effect of the iridescence on the base glass is similar in effect to that of oil spread on water- a rainbow like colouring seen on the surface of the glass, rather than as an integral part of the glass itself.

WHERE WAS CARNIVAL GLASS SOLD?
The short answer must surely be *'worldwide!'* Under the chapter dealing with individual producer-countries there will be detailed reply to this question. We simply note here that internal, as well as external, overseas markets were considered by all the producing companies, even where a limited option was available with Australian Carnival Glass.

Opportunities were sought not only to enlarge markets and thereby sales, but sometimes in an effort to avoid punitive local restrictive trade tariffs (as was the case between Sweden and Norway). There was also considerable liaison (as well as competition) between Glasshouses on an international basis at the time in order to maximise sales. In this way many patterns crossed-over International boundaries, (legitimately or quite the reverse!), following any sales opportunities.

Distribution in America and elsewhere was through various means. Mail Order was popular, as was direct selling through general stores or speciality china outlets. There was even a market for using the ware to harbour such as pickles, jams (jellies) and the like! It even pre-dated the later Depression glass market where it was also offered in Sales Promotions, as prizes through such as furniture stores, sweet and biscuit companies.

WHAT SORT OF PATTERNING, IF ANY, APPEARED ON THIS WARE?
Flora, fauna, naturalistic and geometric patterns abounded! The more intricate, the more they disguised any mould lines or imperfections in the glass or in the manufacture. Favourite designs are discussed for each manufacturer in Chapter Five.

WHY DO WE CALL THIS TYPE OF GLASS 'CARNIVAL GLASS'?
Hereby, a sorry tale of woe! As the markets declined (when tastes and demand changed), the producers were left with large undepleted stock-piles of their iridised pressed glassware.

In desperation it was then off-loaded to Fairs and Carnivals as cheap prizes – at considerable financial loss to the manufacturers, but simply to rid their factories and warehouses of the said stock-piles!

A sad demise for such ware but luckily only of temporary duration since the capricious market forces have now turned full circle and we see prices rising *daily* for this now collectible original ware, as well as a growing popularity for the *New Carnival* that is being produced both in America and in the Far East.

"Plus ça change, plus ça change pas" – as the French would wisely say!

Chapter Two:

Carnival Glass Shapes

SHAPES FOUND IN CARNIVAL GLASS

Carnival Glass was produced to fill a gap in the domestic market where iridised art glass was too expensive a purchase for the average household. Thus any shape that could be used in the home was introduced where practicable. The popularity and success of this ware resulted in a further expansion of design, where the purely decorative was allied to the basically functional possibilities.

The majority production was for BOWL shapes, then PLATES of various sizes along with VASES. As its popularity grew, the ranges on offer by the various manufacturers were expanded in an effort to corner the markets.

Pieces were then adapted to sell as storage containers for such as pickles and jams (jellies) or handed out, appropriately detailed, as advertising pieces or souvenir pieces. In fact, this list could well be practically endless! But here are the BASIC shapes found in this ware, regardless of country of production. The majority are depicted in this book.

Ash-trays	Bon-bon dishes (2 handles)	Covered Butter dishes
Candlesticks	Car vases	Celery Vases
Compotes/coupes	Cookie (biscuit) Jars	Creamers (milk jugs)
Cuspidors aka Spittoons	Dressing table sets	Floral baskets
Epergnes	Flower frogs	Funeral rose bowls
Fruit dessert sets	Jam (Jelly) dishes	Lampshades
Muffin dishes with lid covers	Mugs aka Beakers	Oil Lamps
Paperweights	Pickle dishes	Pintrays
Plates various sizes	Powder bowls with lids	Punch bowl sets
Rose bowls	Sauce boats	Spittoons/Cuspidors
Sugar bowls	Tobacco Jars	Toothpick holders
Tumblers	Vases	Water Sets

and many one-off Whimsey shapes.

PLATES

NB. plates can be collar based or footed:

Collar based: where ideally they are plain-rimmed, not fancy edged, with the edge of the plate standing not more than 2" above its collar base. The plate should be as FLAT as possible.

Footed variety: here the plate surface should be FLAT (otherwise it becomes a footed bowl!). Here the 2" rule noted cannot apply, for obvious reasons.

ICE CREAM BOWLS

These are small, circa 5" diameter maximum and look like shallow bowls in that the edge is slightly and evenly upturned all around the edge.

BASE OR FOOT SHAPES TO CARNIVAL GLASS

There was much variation in the base or foot formation of Carnival glass pieces. We can EASILY find the following:

Collar base – plain rimmed edge, no feet
Knobbed feet – 3 short feet with knob endings
Ball and claw feet – variation on above
Spade/spatula feet – with 3 broad spade-effect feet.
Stubby straight feet – varied in number of feet up to 8
Domed base – with hollow base collar about 1" deep.
These are all depicted in this book.

EDGE SHAPES FOUND ON CARNIVAL GLASS

Again there is a plethora of choice! Hand worked pieces allowed even more variation from the standard edges found on the various shapes. The more intricate or delicate the finish, then the more value can be attributed to the pattern piece. In handworking, the piece would be skillfully drawn out or extended, or crimped or pleated. whilst still hot and just released from the mould. Examples of the various hand-worked edges can be found in this book. Here are some of the most well known :

Pie Crust – Ribbon Candy – Ruffled.

The standard Scallop edge is also shown. This of course was not hand worked, The scallops can also sometimes also be interspersed with smaller raised points.

WELL-KNOWN EDGE SHAPES ON CARNIVAL GLASS

Ribbon Candy edge.

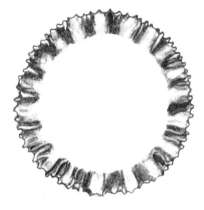

Pie-crust edge.

Ruffled edge.

Scallop edge

Sketches by John Watson

Chapter Three:

Base Glass Colours in Carnival Glass

It is very important to note that in describing the colour of Carnival Glass we refer to the colour of the Base Glass itself and NOT to the colours of the iridescent overlay. Establish the base-glass colour by holding the piece up to the light.

It must also be realised that colours varied in production, and can also vary in the eye of the beholder, so familiarisation with as many colours as possible is the best way to get to know your Carnival Glass, and expand your collection wisely at the same time!

But do not despair at the apparent complexity of it all! It is possible to separate the various colours into four major groupings as follows: **Group One**: Standard colours; **Group Two**: Pastel colours; **Group Three**: Opalescent edge colours; **Group Four**: Rarer base-glass colours

To add to the confusion the names within these groups are not always those used by the original manufacturers but have been universally adopted by collectors.

GROUP ONE: STANDARD COLOURS

Most easily found is Marigold iridescence on clear base glass. Amber – Amethyst – Blue – Green and Red base glass follow on. The red base is by far the rarest and most costly to produce, and is greatly sought after by collectors.

Marigold

The most prolific production was in Marigold on clear flint base. Take care not to confuse this with marigold iridescence over Amber, Yellow or Pink base glass, these are much harder to find!

Marigold iridescence is also found over Milk Glass and even over Green base glass (where it is called Alaskan).

Amber Base Carnival Glass

In America:- Imperial made many pieces in Amber.
– Fenton made less, such as Dragon and Lotus, Vintage, Carnival Holly and Autumn Acorn.
– Northwood pieces have been found in Grape and Cable, Finecut and Roses and Dandelion patterns.
Pale Amber – from USA, Imperial were the main producers.
Honey Amber- again from USA
Deep Amber – from Finland
The Northwood Amber based glass is sometimes called Horehound. where it is a fairly light shade of Amber.

Amber to Red Base Carnival Glass i.e. Amberina

An Amber variation where in the centre of the piece we find a true amber, turning red at the outer edges. These are extremely rare and bring in the highest prices.
There is also a reverse in Red to Amber base Carnival Glass with Red base twirling to Amber.

Amethyst

Here there is a more restricted colour range than with Blue or Green.

Palest Amethyst is: Lavender
Found (though rarely) at Eda Sweden. In USA, there are also rare examples from Dugan, Northwood, Imperial and Millersburg. This may well have been an experimental colour, or simply an off-balance mid amethyst.

Slightly darker: Dugan (USA) produced a delicate, attractive Ribena (blackcurrant cordial colour).

Mid Amethyst: This is the standard, most easily obtained shade.

Black Amethyst: A very popular shade in Australian Production, vying for popularity with Marigold. This looks black until held under a strong light, when the amethyst will come through

Blue

To date, here are the various shades of blue. More seem to be redefined every day! Mid blue is the least expensive and not hard to track down as it was produced in quantity.

Palest blue is: Ice Blue
Slightly darker: Celeste Blue
Darker again: Sapphire Blue or a summer sky blue Teal Blue (similar to Sapphire Blue but with green overtones)
then: Mid Blue (the most easy to find)
thereafter: Persian Blue (this is actually Blue Moonstone)
lastly (to date!):   Renniger Blue akin to Teal but with stronger blue

Teal Blue has been found with the Imperial Waffle Block pattern, also with Westmoreland's Scales and Coin Dot.

Electric Blue Carnival is named after the Brilliance of the iridisation process. The term Electric with regard to carnival can therefore also be applied to other base-glass colours with a similar iridescence over.

Green

There are as many variations for Green as for Blue based Carnival Glass. Mid Green is the cheapest as most easily found.

Palest green is: Ice Green and gentle iridescence
slightly darker: Lime Green and a yellow tint
darker again: Emerald Green (with a blue tinge)
then: Mid Green (the most easy to find)
next: Nile Green and Russet Green (with an olive tinge)
                        Teal Green

There is also a marigold iridescence over green from the American ware, called Alaska
Care must be taken not to confuse the paler shades of green based ware with Vaseline Based Carnival Glass , which is smeared greeny-yellow, akin to Petroleum Jelly!

Red Base Carnival Glass

Up till now, this base glass colour has always attracted the highest prices, as so very rare and difficult to produce, with expensive gold oxides used in the manufacturing process.

But as awareness of rarities grows, red base glass now faces stiff competition as to value! There are already other competitors jostling for "Top Dollar" – namely the rarer-based iridised glass pieces: such as Jet Glass base/Crackle base/Slag and Custard base ware etc. These are often single or limited production experimental pieces and as such are very much sought after. It looks as if these are already competing for highest value with red and amberina based Carnival Glass.

GROUP TWO – PASTELS IN CARNIVAL GLASS

These were mainly produced by the American companies, though some examples exist in the various Continental, English and Scandinavian areas. Expect these to attain higher prices than the standard deeper colours, with a further increase in value where they also have opalescent edges.

Apricot   Just like the fruit!
Butterscotch   This is a very soft pale gold iridescence over clear base glass.
Citrene   pale lemon-yellow
Champagne   as the wine!
Clear   self explanatory
Ice Blue   see under Blue
Ice Green   see under Green
                     Can also be found with a marigold iridescence over instead of the usual clear iridescent spray.

Lavender	– Northwood used this colour, though sparingly. There is a Northwood (USA) Good Luck Bowl as example.
	– Millersburg (USA) has a valuable Trout And Fly piece
	– Dugan pieces such as Dogwood Sprays, Wishbone and Leaf And Beads.
	– There is also a rare example of this delicate base colour with a Swedish Four Flowers Variant bowl.
Pastel Horehound	Pale Amber
Pastel Marigold	also called Butterscotch
Pearl Carnival	This is actually Iridised Custard where a clear iridescence over has been used.
Pink	A soft delicate pink. This is a rare-base- glass for Carnival. The Finnish Glasshouses used this base colour, naming it RIO. A marigold iridescence was used ,(there is a Finnish exterior Crackle pattern Bowl with Four Flowers interior on RIO base).
Smoke	Light grey. Usually Imperial USA, but some pieces were produced in limited quantity by Northwood (such as Peacock on the Fence pattern) and some by Fenton as well.
White	(i) A frosted translucent white with a gentle iridescence over.
	(ii) Opaque white, Milk glass base, with iridesence over (clear or marigold).
Yellow	Often found on Four Flowers and Variants, some of these known to come from Sweden (EDA). EDA used yellow quite extensively as a base glass colour for pressed and blown ware.
	The patterns Poppy Show and Rose Show have also appeared in this base colour. It is thought these hail from Westmoreland USA but this has to be proven.

These pastel shades are rarer than standard base colours, and were made mainly in America, though some are found in Sweden also in England and the then-named early Czechoslovakia.

GROUP THREE – OPALESCENT EDGE

This is glass that has been in part, re-heated to provide an opalescent ribbon-like edge to the piece whatever the basic glass colour or iridescent overlay. To date, examples have only been found on American production ware, Dugan producing the majority.

Such an edging can appear on Standard base colour Carnival Glass and also, (though less frequently) on Pastel or the Rare-base-glass Carnival. This since we are dealing here not only with a base-glass, iridised over, but also with the effect of reheating the glass at the edge, which results in the opaque chalky-white ribbon band edge already explained.

To date, only pieces produced in America have been found. Here are the best-known base-glass colours with opalescent edge:

Amethyst Opalescent	Milkglass Opalescent milk glass base
Aqua Opalescent a soft sea-green base colour	Peach Opalescent
Blue Opalescent	Pearl Opalescent
Lime Opalescent	Vaseline Opalescent
Marigold Opalescent	White Opalescent

GROUP FOUR – RARER-BASE-GLASS COLOURS

These occur where the iridisation process is applied to other than flint pressed glass,- to such as Milk Glass, Slag Glass, Jet Glass, Custard Glass, Moonstone Glass, Crackle Glass, Cranberry Glass and Vaseline Glass.

These always attract premium prices and can supersede Red Base Carnival Glass in attracting the highest interest and value. Definition of the base glass type and colour is therefore an essential factor in determining rarity and value for any piece of Carnival Glass.

Some pieces with rare base-glass can be found with Opalescent edge treatment as well, increasing their desirability even further amongst collectors! Such glass appeared in non-iridised form long before the Carnival Glass period and the pieces that have appeared iridised are RARE, possibly experimental as regards technique or were produced to test the market.

The collector must also realise that growing awareness, coupled with the results of increased research as well as expanding interest in this ware, have together resulted in a quite complex listing and separation of the various shades of each base-glass colour. Many are found in the USA only.

It is therefore essential to see and handle as much Carnival Glass as possible in order to familiarise oneself with all the various collectible colours (and shades of colour).

Awareness of possible market price variations must also apply to all buying and selling of Carnival Glass. So, "Caveat Emptor" – 'Let the buyer beware' – colours and shapes and patterns can go out of fashion as easily as they become sought after!

Here follows a detailed guide into the basic range of Carnival Glass base-colours and their relative values. The colours given are as named in America.

Iridised Amberina and Reverse Amberina Glass
Amberina is Red based glass with a colouring-off to yellow.

The lighter shade tending to be found in the centre of the piece. With reverse amberina, we have the opposite colour play. This glass was the product of specific heating techniques.

Iridised Black Amethyst Glass
Outwardly this has the appearance of Iridised Jet Glass. But if held up to a very strong light, then a deep amethyst colour shows through the black base glass.

This was very popular in Australian production , though rarer elsewhere.

Iridised Chocolate Glass
This is known only from American production to date.

Iridised Crackle Glass
There are a few examples of blow-moulded pressed crackle glassware with marigold iridescence over. These are extremely rare. See the example in this book: Enamelled Clematis. Fenton in USA has produced a recent range of Crackle Iridised ware each piece clearly marked on its base.

Iridised Cranberry Glass
Known in USA as Cranberry Flash.

Iridised Custard Glass
Standard custard glass (opaque and cream coloured glass) with iridescent overlay. The majority of this was made by Northwood but all pieces are rare and much sought after. Patterns such as Poppy, Grape and Cable, Tree Trunk Vase and Beaded Cable have all been found on such ware.

It is also worth noting that the term Pearl Carnival relates to Iridised Custard Glass where a Clear overspray has been used instead of a marigold iridisation.

Iridised Jet Glass
Produced at Riihimaki, Finland(though rarely); Sowerby, England (extremely rare); and Dugan USA though not in great quantity.

The only known Sowerby pattern to date on Iridised Jet Glass is the Cynthia Vase. This in an attractive Art Deco shape Vase, most probably experimental production since practically only a few examples found. A collector's dream! This Vase can have either a flared or a turned-in top rim.

Expect to pay highest prices for such pieces, from whichever source.

Iridised Milk Glass
1. Opaque, and either chalk-white or white with a blue tint. Both types with a clear iridescence over. Fenton produced many pieces in this glass.
2. There is also a marigold iridescence over milk glass, known as Iridised Marigold Milk Glass.
3. There is also a Smoke Iridised Milk Glass.

Iridised Moonstone Glass
Akin to Milk Glass but semi-opaque whereby light can shine through the base when held up to view.
   This was a favourite of Fenton, who clearly used the name on their products in this range. Patterns found with this glass base include Orange Tree Bowl, Dragon and Lotus, Peacock and Grape and also Peacock and Urn.
   Iridised blue moonstone pieces are sometimes called Persian Blue.

Iridised Rio Glass (ie Pink based glass)
This was used at the Finnish glassworks, usually with a strong marigold iridescence over. (Refer also to notes under Pastels)

Iridised Slag Glass
There is of course a variety of base glass colours for slag and some of these are iridised, though "one-offs".

Iridised Stretch Glass
Quite a few pieces appear in American production , such as Imperial's Jewels Vase, but Czechoslovakian manufacture appears the most prominent.

Iridised Vaseline Glass
This is a true greeny-yellow colour base glass with marigold iridised overlay and was produced in limited quantity by:
– Northwood USA: with such as Concave Diamond Water Pitcher, Hearts and Flowers Plate.
– Millersburg USA: with, for example, the Holly Sprig, Night Stars and Peacock and Urn patterns.
– Fenton USA: the majority producer, with patterns such as the Peacock and Grape and Hat shape bowls appearing quite regularly. There is also a very rare and valuable Blackberry Block Water Pitcher.
– Czechoslovakian manufacture: the rare and very large Art Deco style Pebble and Fan Vase is to be found on Vaseline base, with marigold iridescence over.
– There appears to have been no production in UK or in Scandinavian countries.

IRIDISATION FINISHES: (I-IV)
The iridisation finish can be varied on Carnival Glass. The variations are usually grouped as follows and can affect the value of the ware:

(i) Electric Finish
A quite brilliant and spectacular finish, found on such as Blue, Amethyst, Green and Marigold base Carnival Glass.

(ii) Satin Finish
A soft finish, with a gentle all-over iridescence. There is often a metallic (silver or gold) effect introduced. A regular favourite with Northwood (USA) production.

(iii) Radium
A different iridescence in that, although brilliant and sparkling it is also Translucent allowing the base glass colour to show through in normal light. A good example on Green base is the Millersburg Mayan bowl.

(iv) Alaskan
Where Northwood used a Marigold iridescence over green base glass – an unusual rather bronze effect was produced. Patterns known with this iridescence include such as Daisy and Plume, and Wild Roses.
NB Early producers often advertised their ware by describing the colour effect of the Iridisation rather than the colour of the Base Glass.

Chapter Four

A Brief History of American Carnival Glass Production

1920s early Carnival, 1960s Reproduction Carnival and New Carnival (Modern).

Early Carnival Glass

In the 1880s the American Glasshouses developed a *hand operated mechanical* manufacturing process that enabled them to produce glassware in vast quantities at an inexpensive price. This was through the introduction of hand operated press moulds, rather than from using the old established, but costly technique of hand blowing glass.

This opened up a whole new era of glass production – the semi mechanised technique could now be used to imitate the far more costly crystal glass manufacturing procedures. It was expected that the general public would be only too pleased to be able to buy their domestic glassware at considerably less cost than previously possible. This glass followed the old traditional crystal glass in that it was clear (not coloured) and retained the heavy geometric designs. It was an immediate success.

By the turn of the century however, it was realised that this market could be further expanded:
1) by applying *iridisation* to the surface of the glass
2) by offering various *Base Colours* in the glass itself (as opposed to the flint glass previously only available). The techniques for iridisation were already to hand following the iridised blown art glass from such established experts as Louis Comfort Tiffany
3) by applying naturalistic and geometric designs rather than remaining solely with the old crystal ware cuts.
4) by enlarging the product range to cover as many domestic table-ware or decorative items as possible.

The manufacturers were also quick to realise that the semi-opacity of such ware would allow for cost savings in the manufacturing techniques, and that the many intricate patterns on offer would also camouflage any impurities or blemishes in the finished product.

All these factors came together to provide a sure-fire commercial success. And these were further supported by the population explosion in America during the late nineteenth century, where every household sought to improve its standard of living, and where retail markets were booming

Sales were instigated through cheap dime stores, such as Woolworths, as well as through up-market china and glass ware sales outlets, and via mail-order catalogues. This ware was sold by the barrel load throughout USA and exported to England and Australia as well.

Page 15 shows an article about Imperial Iridised pressed patterned ware in the UK which appeared in the *Pottery Gazette* (1st March 1911). As the reader will note, the names given to the various pieces do *not* equate to the description we would ally to these pieces nowadays though the term 'Helios' is still recognised. The description here relates to the iridescent finish, not to the base-glass shades.

Unfortunately, this booming market came to a sudden end in the late 1920s when public taste veered in favour of the newly emerging Art deco design influences. Faced with huge stocks of unsold ware, the suppliers off-loaded their goods to such as Travelling Fairs and Amusement Arcades. Here it was offered as cheap prizes, earning the then rather derogatory title of Carnival Glass.

This was a sad demise for a fine product. Since its inception it had played the role of honest broker in marrying together commercially both the old techniques of iridisation and hand working of glass with the most modern press moulding procedures available at the time. Carnival glass was produced in vast quantities, press-moulded, but often hand-worked at the edges or hand swung to extend the shape so it still retained individuality within the inexpensive mass production techniques. It was a brave experiment that has lasted the test of time, since nowadays such glass has become very collectable and admired worldwide.

The innovative techniques employed and the complexity of allying old with new remains as a prime example of the imaginative, industrious and skilled inventiveness of the glassmaker.

The American methods for producing Carnival Glass

This was *not* hand blown glass. It was machine pressed, using hand operated press-moulds. This allowed for inexpensive production suitable for mass sale at low cost. Although made in the mould, a certain individuality could be applied where pieces could be hand-worked and varied in shape as they left the mould, and whilst still hot. According to the skill of the worker, we can find such as pieces with ruffled or pleated edges, turned over lips, pulled or stretched vases.

Various-coloured base glass was used and there is now a complicated list of colours defined by modern collectors of the ware. Each has its own value, some such as Red or Jet being extremely rare and most sought after. The Red since it required *gold* in the manufacturing process, the Jet because of its extreme rarity in the

Pottery Gazette *1st March 1911: An article re USA Imperial iridised pressed glassware.*

Carnival Glass world of colours (it came at the end of Carnival Glass era, entering the Art Deco World, and was mainly limited experimental production).

The roles of mould maker, glass handler and worker operating the press were all crucial to production. The apparatus used demanded a changeable metal mould with a plunger above, which could be thrust down into the mould to control the flow of glass. The mould itself had to be of good quality for a clear impression to be produced.

The iridisation essential to Carnival Glass was produced by coating the glass with metallic salts – these added *after* the initial firing. The ware was then 're-fired' – to set the iridescence.

At some glasshouses, the iridisation was sprayed on, at others brushed. Each manufacturer sought to develop his own formulae for the various iridisation effects, and the ware was variously described as such as Taffeta Glass, Aurora Glass, New Venetian or Etruscan ware. Some such names were then variously redefined by Agents abroad and this adds to the confusion. Included in this chapter are an article and an advertisement from the English *Pottery Gazette* of 1st March 1911, relating to the marketing of Imperial USA ware through the agent Markt & Co.

Since the modern collector collects by *base-glass* colour, *not* by colour effect of the applied iridescence, this has resulted in some confusion over the exact definition of colour in relation to the Manufacturers involved.

As for the Patterns used in Carnival Glass production, these mainly followed the Art Nouveau artistic ideal. Flora and fauna, and indeed all naturalistic patterns abounded.

Each pattern was extremely intricate and a test of skill for the mould maker. Some Manufacturers however, (and Imperial comes instantly to mind) preferred to remain with the detailed geometric cuts reminiscent of more costly blown crystal ware.

American producers of Early Carnival Glass
Apart from the five major producers discussed later there were various *limited* producers of Carnvial Glass in America in the early part of the century. The most well known are noted herewith:
Cambridge Glass Co-Ohio
Columbia Glass Co
Fostoria of West Virginia
Heisey of Newark Ohio
Jenkins Glass Co of Kokomo Indiana:
Mckee Jeanette of Jeanette Pennsylvania
as well as US Glass of Pittsburgh, Pennsylvania.
   Some examples of their production of Carnival Glassware are given in this book.

   We meanwhile turn to the history of the *FIVE* **INTERNATIONALLY RECOGNISED** *MAJOR* **PRODUCERS OF CARNIVAL GLASS WARE IN THE UNITED STATES OF AMERICA** at the start of this century. These are Dugan, Fenton, Imperial, Millersburg and Northwood, and they will be discussed in some depth in this chapter. An outline of their production history is noted. These five major producers are described as follows:

Dugan

The Dugan Glass Company actually began producing glass in Indiana Pennsylvania in 1892 (in a region with a tradition of fine glassmaking), when it traded under the name The Indiana Glass Company. This Company was short lived and closed down just one year later. It was then taken over on lease by Harry Northwood, already operating at Ellwood City PA as one of America's leading glassmakers of the era. He shared ownership of the Northwood Glass Company with his wife Clara and with Thomas and Anne Dugan (his Uncle and Aunt).
   The new site at Indiana produced until 1895, when Northwood moved out. He left the plant in the charge of the previous Managers W G Minnemeyer and his Uncle Thomas E Dugan. They changed the name to the Dugan Glass Company and continued to produce ware along the established Northwood lines. Harry Northwood had brought in many moulds and most of these were left to be re-worked. The Dugan ware was marked with a capital D inside a Diamond shape, often on old Northwood moulds.
In 1913 the glass company changed its name to the Diamond Glass Company and Thomas Dugan continued to oversee the production.
   According to local newspapers and trade journals, Dugan began to produce a fine array of both domestic and decorative glassware. Items as various as lampshades, condiment sets, tableware sets, dressing table sets, as well as the standard bowls, water sets and storage syrups, were all made.
   Unfortunately the factory took fire in 1931 and was never rebuilt as any probable output was threatened by economic problems during the Great Depression.
   For Carnival Glass collectors, Dugan produced a vast quantity of iridised pressed ware with opalescent edges. The patterns listed below are all from this source, and reflect the excellence of design and workmanship found here in Indiana.

Apple Blossom Twigs	Beaded shell	Beaded Panels
Beauty Twig Vase	Big Basketweave Vase	Blossom & Band Car vase
Border plants	Butterfly and Tulip	Cherry
Cherry... Wreathed cherry	Circled Scroll	Coin Spot
Compass (ext pattern)	Cosmos Variant	Dogwood Sprays
Double Stem Rose	Crackle Car Vase	Fan
Fanciful	Farmyard	Fisherman's Mug
Fishnet	Floral & Grape	Floral and Wheat
Flowers & Frames	Flowers & Spades	Folding Fan

Formal	Four Flowers	Garden path vrnt
Grape & Cable(Dugan version)	Grapevine Lattice	Heavy Grape
Heavy Iris Water set	Heavy Webb	Jewelled Heart
Leaf Rays	Lined Lattice	Many Fruits
Maple Leaf	Nautilus	Pastel Swans
Peach and Pear	Peacock at the Fountain	Persian Garden
Petals & Fans	Puzzle	Question Marks
Quill Water set	Raindrops	Round-up
Single Flower	Six Petals	Ski-star
Soutache	Spiralex Vase	Starfish Stippled
Rambler Rose	Stork & Rushes	Target Vase
Vineyard	Vining Twigs	Vintage
Windflower	Wishbone and Spades	

The Windflower pattern is found quite frequently in the UK on basic bowls. Apple Blossom Twigs Punch cups and the Maple Leaf compote are also quite readily available, along with Double Stemmed Rose. All are found in marigold or amethyst.

Fenton

Fenton was the first of the large scale American Carnival Glass producers and still continues the Carnival Glass tradition today, along with the production of other fine art glassware.

The Fenton Art Glass Company was started up in 1906 by two brothers, Frank L Fenton and his brother John, at Martins Ferry Ohio, in the heart of the glass producing area. By 1907 a new plant had been designed and completed at Williamstown West Virginia and the complex, much extended, is still there today. Below is an early postcard photograph of the site.

THE NEW FENTON GLASS FACTORY AF WILLIAMSTOWN W.VA.

From the outset Frank Fenton exhibited a natural flair for anticipating market forces, and this attribute, coupled with a considerable ability for design soon attracted buyers and general public to his glassworks. The iridised pressed ware was immensely popular and Frank Fenton also benefited from the assistance of Jacob Rosenthal, a glassmaking genius who came direct from the now defunct Indiana Tumbler and Goblet Company to assist in production.

In 1908 the two brothers fell out and John departed to form the Millersburg Glass Company. The public clamoured for the Fenton Carnival Glassware, with its imaginative designs and quality product offered at a very low price. This happy state of affairs was to continue for 15 years – and the iridised ware output far exceeded any other production lines at Fenton.

Over 150 patterns can definitely be attributed to Fenton over the Carnival Glass period, and doubtless more will be so defined as research continues.

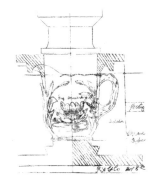

The glass was sold by the barrel load throughout the dime store, glass retail outlets and more up-market sales venues in the USA as well as exported far afield to UK and Australia.

The Fenton Glass Company has continued to thrive over the years and still produces Carnival Glass today. This modern Carnival Glass is clearly named on the base of each piece with a Logo as depicted here.

Such ware is collected worldwide and its popularity never appears to wane. Fenton has a superb Museum and a Retail Glass Sales Shop outlet and also produces special limited edition ware in pressed iridised form. Some designs reflect those of the earliest Carnival Glass ware, others are new- all are extremely collectable.

Below is a photograph of the pot-setters at the early Fenton works, followed by a blue-print reproduction for a Tiger Lily mould.

A recent production has been for *Iridised Blow-Moulded Crackle Glass* as depicted in the catalogue reprint on page 83. The crackle glass treatment is achieved by the hand blown process. Molten glass is gathered at the end of a hollow blow pipe. Then it is placed in cool water, to fracture the outer surface of

Below: The author with Howard Seufer (Fenton Glass photographer for this book) at the Fenton Glass Museum in 1996; and right: the author with Frank Fenton at the same location.

the glass. It is then re-heated to seal the cracks.

This procedure can be repeated up to three times for larger pieces. The glass is then *blown into the final forming mould* and an iridised finish is applied. Whilst this is not strictly Carnival Glass (it lacks the traditional patterning and press moulding in toto) it is still of interest to collectors as it extends their collecting.

Fenton continues the tradition of making pressed iridised glass for special orders. Here is a modern *Loving Cup* on iridised custard glass, made for the Heart of America Carnival Glass Association.

Below follow some Fenton Catalogue entries from the recent production lines of New Carnival Glass. See page 83 for further colour examples of this ware.

Imperial

The principal glass-producing region of the United States at the start of this century was situated on either side of the Ohio River. Here Imperial set up a glasshouse in 1904, in direct competition with established glasshouses such as Northwood and the National Glass Factory. It obviously believed in the premise that competition attracts trade!

From the outset it specialised in geometric and near-cut patterns rather than naturalistic patterns, and favoured useful practical glassware rather than decorative ware for its output. In this way it offered an alternative market from the other glasshouses such as Fenton. By 1909 it had realised the success of Fenton's <u>iridised</u> pressed ware and sought to enter this field as well.

Such was the quality of its production that success was almost immediately assured, even though competitors such as Millersburg and Dugan were also taking up such lines. Fenton ware sold well throughout the United States and overseas in vast quantity at very low prices. Imperial also tapped overseas export markets, through such agents as Markt and Co Ltd of London. Sowerby of UK paid Imperial the ultimate compliment by copying the 'Scroll Emboss' Imperial pattern, and Eda Glassworks of Sweden copied and extended the Imperial range of the 'Tiger Lily' and 'Curved Star' patterns (as did Finnish and Estonian Glasshouses). Imperial ware also reached Central and South American countries and even Australia. For the sales of Imperial ware in Australia, there may have been a UK intermediary.

A BRILLIANT AND UNUSUAL IRIDESCENCE WAS THE HALLMARK OF IMPERIAL'S SUCCESS. There was also the development of more unusual base glass colours such as Smoke and Clambroth. The smoke colour was originally referred to as Sapphire and no other producer

Imperial Reproduction Carnival Glass Catalogue Entries.

managed to make an equivalent shade. The Acanthus Plate is often found on Smoke base glass. Clambroth was a pale ginger-ale colour and is very much sought after by collectors of this old Imperial pressed iridised ware. Amber was another colour favoured by Imperial, though floral designs were mainly produced in this shade rather than geometric patterns.

There were also three shades of green glass:

Helios: where the light green base glass has a quite distinctive gold/silver metallic iridescence

Emerald: an extremely hard-to find brilliant base glass colour

Mid Green: with a rather metallic and multi-coloured iridescence.

Imperial 'marigold' was produced in vast quantities and the Imperial 'purple' was strong and deep, and was never surpassed by any competitors. Red was produced only in minute quantities, possibly to special order, likewise White and Cobalt blue and the pastels (vaseline base, and olive, lavender, teal, ice blue and green, aqua and violet).

In 1910 the Company introduced another innovation with its 'stretch' glass – often found iridised under the Imperial Jewels range. By 1922 a line of unusual hand blown crystal cased coloured glassware was in production, sometimes iridised. Glass artists had been brought from Europe to advise on this range and many such pieces reflect pieces produced at Eda in Sweden, during its own lustre ware production period.

Unfortunately with the advent of the Great Depression, the glasshouses fell into financial difficulties. Imperial managed to soldier on by using many of the old Carnival Glass moulds to produce inexpensive Depression Ware glass in pink, blue and green. The struggle to survive was rewarded with expansion in 1940-1960 and moulds were supplemented with buying in from the now defunct Heisey and Cambridge Glass companies.

In 1962 there was a nostalgic resurgence of interest in the old iridised pressed glassware of the 1920s and Imperial was not slow to realise the sales potential in this matter. It re-produced iridised pressed glass Carnival Ware from the old moulds, though usually, but not always, changing the base glass colours.

This 1960s reproduction ware is now also very collectable as Imperial sank into a slow decline in the 1970s following a buy-out and several failed private ventures on the site. By 1985 all production had stopped, despite a late attempt at resuscitation by a group of four glass artisans trading under the short- lived name of The Pioneer Glass Company.

The various Reproduction Carnival Glass lines came out between 1962 up to as late as 1981. Colour names were advertised as follows (actual colour follows after):

Rubigold (marigold), *Peacock* (smoke), *Helios Green*

Red: Pansy, Fieldflower, Robin Mug, Lustre Rose, Diamond Lace, Octagon patterns all feature in this base-glass colour.

Azure (ice blue), *Aurora Jewels* (cobalt).

White: Amber, Meadow Green (emerald), *Pink.*
Horizon Blue, Amethyst.

Imperial used several trademarks throughout its long working life and these are noted below *covering the various ownerships* over the two production periods for Carnival Glass.

Above: Trademarks used between 1951-1982. Left: 1951-1972. Centre: as IGC Liquidating Corporation, 1973-1981, and right Arthur Lorch ownership, 1981-1982.
Left: Trademarks used between 1905-1921.

Some examples of the ware produced during this 1960s second period are shown here so that readers can familiarise themselves with the various patterns that identify Imperial Carnival Glass from this era. Specific orders were also made for such as the International Carnival Glass Association and the American Carnival Glass Association.

Millersburg

Millersburg factory was starred up by John Fenton, brother and partner of Frank Fenton of the Fenton Art Glass Company. John wanted to prove his own ability following the success of the joint venture at Fenton. This decision was to benefit later collectors with the output from Millerburg Glass.

John set up a new factory site at Millersburg in Holmes County Ohio. The local people, including the Amish who lived in the area welcomed the stranger and adopted his plans as their own. The new Glasshouse offered work and the prospect of some security for them.

By 1909 the new and purpose built factory was ready. The plant prospered for a good four years, but gradually the stiff competition was to overwhelm the genius, but weak, business sense of the owner. Artistic ability was insufficient to maintain a durable and viable economic status in such a competitive field. Financial disaster struck in the spring of 1911 when John finally faced the reality that expenditure did not balance with income. The factory was then sold to Samuel Fair who kept it running under the name of The Radium Glass Company. But this change of ownership did not prosper either, the factory finally closed down for good in 1913, the site sold to the Forrester Tire and Rubber Company.

We are left with a legacy of superb workmanship, design and quality. John Fenton had designed his own moulds, including 'Ohio Star' and 'Hobstar and Feather' as his initial ventures. He had already designed the 'Goddess of the Harvest' bowl at Fenton Art Glass Company and this remains one of the prime pieces in the Carnival Glass world even today.

The glass produced at Millersburg was of top quality crystal and the iridised pressed ware included a soft marigold, an amethyst and a green base glass. The success of the new moulds lead to the introduction of more patterns including the Multi Fruits and Flowers design. By the start of 1910, Millerburg glasshouse was able to offer a new *Radium* finish to its pressed iridised ware. This was unique in its beauty, with a softer shade of colour in this finish than previously available. It also had a mirror like finish on the front of the glass. This was an immediate success, so much so that it was soon copied by rival Glasshouses such as Imperial.

A now famous Commemorative Bowl was produced in 1910. It was named the Courthouse Bowl and was in effect a tribute to the workers who had laid the initial gas lines to the factory complex. Moulds from Hipkins Bros produced such as the Country Kitchen, Poppy, Diamond, Rosalind and Pipe Humidor patterns, and the Peacock patterns which remain firm favourites to this day.

Northwood

Harry Northwood founded the Northwood Glass Company at Martins Ferry Ohio in 1887, at the early age of only 27 years. He was one of ten children of the renowned English glassmaker John Northwood. Harry had served a traditional glassmaking apprenticeship in England. He arrived in the United States of America at the age of 21 years, probably in the company of his relative Thomas Dugan, who was also to become a major Carnival Glass producer later on.

Harry worked for various glasshouses before starting up on his own. His Company was not slow to prosper, his glassmaking genius and artistic ability saw to that. By 1892 he had moved to a new purpose built factory in Ellwood City. But business in the glass trade was extremely competitive, and Harry was obliged to close down and move several times before he set up his final production base at the old Hobbs Brockunier factory in Wheeling W Virginia in 1902.

Late in 1907 Fenton Art Glass astounded the markets with its newly introduced iridised coloured pressed glassware. Harry Northwood decided to enter the same field. Using moulds from earlier pressed glass he rushed out a line in marigold Carnival, naming it Golden Iris. Other base glass colours followed, purple green and cobalt blue were next on line. New patterns such as Fine Cut & Roses, Beaded Cable and Wild Rose all appeared at this juncture.

In 1910 the Grape and Cable Design was introduced- to immense and immediate sales. By 1912 the pastel range followed- these we now refer to as White, Ice Green and Ice Blue. The output in new patterns was equally prolific, over 100 were developed with new moulds introduced. The Grape and Cable Design (which was to prove the biggest seller of all) was offered to a discerning public in around 70 shapes alone! This was later copied by both Dugan and Fenton- a true accolade for its popularity.

All this expansion was costly and by 1912 Northwood settled for a period of consolidation. The new designs of Acorn Burrs, Nippon, Peacock and Urn and Peacock at the Fountain, amongst many others, enjoyed continuing success and sales. In 1915 a Custard glass iridised range appeared, followed two years after that by a line of iridised stretch glass.

With the Iridised Custard Glass, patterns such as Fine cut and Roses, Singing Birds, Three Fruits, Grape Arbor (all bearing a light pastel iridescence) made their appearance. There was also experimental production of a deeper marigold iridescence on Custard Glass, but this was not followed up in any quantity. Unfortunately all this effort came to a sudden end when Harry developed a fatal illness, dying in 1918. His Company carried on, but without his genius for design and his flair for trade, slipped into a slow commercial decline till it finally closed in 1925.

Northwood Trademarks

The Northwood Glass Company employed the following trademark from 1905 and this regularly appears on Carnival Glass from this early period.

Unfortunately, the trademark noted left has been somewhat abused in New Carnival Glass production. To clarify this point, we show two other similar trademarks and their origins on the following page (where they do *not* actually represent the earlier Northwood manufacture).

L G Wright Glass Co

Used by L G Wright in the 1970s and applied to old Dugan/Diamond moulds purchased after the works was destroyed by fire in the 1930s. Its similarity to the old Northwood moulds mark caused great confusion with collectors and was eventually dropped. L G Wright now uses a W within a circle for its trademark for iridised pressed NEW Carnival glassware.

Mosser Glass Co

This mark appeared on *New Carnival Glass* in the early 1980s and again was too close to the original Northwood Trademark for comfort! At the time the copyright to the Northwood original was owned by the American Carnival Glass Association who took legal action to suppress the use of this misleading trademark – and succeeded! Mosser now use a trademark of an "M" inside a circle for its *New* Carnival Glass.

Rare colours in Northwood Carnival Glass

Northwood produced *no* true *Red Base Carnival Glass* since development of this shade by Fenton and Imperial followed *after* Harry Northwood's demise.

Vivid colours are quite abundant in Northwood production, the pastels (with their later production) less easily found and therefore more costly for modern day collectors. White is more easily found than Pastels Blue or Green, as is Amber.

Colours such as Lavender, Black Amethyst, Teal, Renniger Blue, Vaseline and Horehound, Smoke, Aqua, Pearl (on custard glass), Olive and Lime Green are all very difficult to find and rare

Peach Opalescent was an exploratory experimental colour and therefore extremely rare in the Northwood production. This is actually marigold Carnival with a white opalescent edge band. Dugan is the largest producer of this type of Carnival Glass.

Northwood made more Aqua Opalescent than his competitors. Its rarity lies in the fact this formula was probably brought, or bought into Northwood Glass Company originally from outside. There are no trade references attributing its development to Northwood, despite the output. A few rare items appear with a Northwood signature – and these are the rarities to look out for. Perhaps Northwood turned to production of this colour WITHIN the works at some stage under his own name?

Confusion over Dugan and Northwood Patterns

It has been established by researchers such as the late Bill Heacock that when Northwood left his factory in Indiana he left many moulds behind. These were taken up with the Thomas Dugan Carnival Glass production lines **after** 1908.

Patterns that can now be definitely attributed to Dugan/Diamond and *not* to Northwood are as follows: Butterfly and Tulip; Many Fruits; Farmyard Bowl; Fan; Jewelled Hearts; Victorian; S-Repeat; Nautilus; Maple Leaf; Grape Arbor Bowl; Wreathed Cherry

Northwood use of moulds from Jefferson of Follansbee

Research is still continuing in America by Carl O Burns and others into the use of some Jefferson moulds by Northwood.

Jefferson patterns were made in Carnival Glass by Northwood:

Finecut and Roses Footed Bowl; Meander as external pattern on Three Fruits, Sunflower, Grape & Cable; Vintage – external pattern found on Star of David and Bows, Octet and Three Fruits; Ruffles and Rings – external pattern to Wishbone and Rosette.

Later production Carnival Glass in America

Whilst it is quite impossible to cover the extensive history of Carnival Glass ware as reproduced **after** the 1920s, see pages 82 and 83 for some catalogue entries to give the reader a GENERAL idea as to the type of ware available from this period from L E Smith and from the Indiana Glass Company as well as the Fenton Art Glass Company.

Chapter Five

Non American Producer Countries

In alphabetical order of Country.

The major producer countries outside of America, as known to date: America, Argentina, Australia, Czechoslovakia, England, Estonia, Finland and Sweden. Research is also under way regarding possible Russian production.

These countries all took up production of *iridised pressed ware* in their own glasshouses following the American success of its Carnival Glassware sales. They had already seen the effect of the American Carnival Glassware on their own internal markets and were determined to try and effect sales from their own output.

New machinery had already been brought in to modernise the various Glassworks following invention of the steam presses, and pressed glass manufacture was well established. So it was not a great step to move on to *iridised pressed ware*, or *pressed lustre ware* as the Europeans called this glass.

Patterns differed from the American, both for the chance to expand on any sales potential as well as to cater for localised preferences. All the works were familiar with iridisation techniques from earlier blown glass production.

There was never the mass of manufacture as in USA, nor the development of the more exotic base-glass colours, but each country nevertheless managed to produce 'Carnival Glass' to compete on local markets with the influx of the American imported ware.

We now move on to discuss these production outputs, in alphabetical order of country.

Argentina

A limited production of some pieces of iridised pressed ware have surfaced in the United States of America and have been traced to the Regolleau Cristalleros Co of Buenos Aires. The Beetle Ashtray is one such pattern. Little further is known at this time.

Australia

Carnival Glass was exported to Australia from America, Fenton being the major importer though some American Carnival Glass appears to have arrived indirectly via UK Agents. The Australian Company Crystal Glassworks of Sydney Australia initiated its own production in 1918, specialising in producing patterns that reflected the local native flora and fauna. Bowls and Water sets were the most usual production, though Cake plates, Float bowls and flower frogs, along with table items such as sugar and creamer sets were also introduced.

The quality of design was excellent and this was often complemented by an unusual black-amethyst base glass. This was so dark as to appear black unless held up to a very strong light, when the amethyst then became obvious. Items were also made on clear (flint) with a marigold overlay. There does *not* appear to have been any persistent use of Pastel Shades in base glass, though the odd *Emu* bowl has surfaced in *Aqua*. Nor was any glass apparently produced with an opalescent edge finish as popular in America, especially with Dugan.

Some rarer pieces appear in flint glass, with an iridised marigold spray applied to the *base* of the glass, intaglio set. The *Diana* bowl is one such highly collectable piece, the *Australian Pansy* another. These were supplied from Sweden (Eda Glasshouse) and were apparently iridised upon arrival in Australia. The original *Diana* bowl (non-iridised) is found in Sweden and appears in the *Eda* glass catalogues.

The photograph at the top of the next page shows such a non-iridised *Diana* Bowl, taken from the Eda (Sweden) production range. This bowl was part of a set consisting of 6 small shallow bowls, with straight sides and a larger matching Master Bowl as portrayed here.

The intaglio (ie recessed) design can be found on Australian ware in Marigold iridised form.

The Australian Crystal Glassworks later amalgamated with the Australian Glass Manufacturers Company (AGM) via a series of mergers with other companies. Records still available through the AGM establish that Australian Carnival Glass ware was first manufactured circa 1922-23 and possibly a little later, was taken up by the Crystal Glassworks of Windham Street, Waterloo, Sydney.

The Crystal Glass Company was founded in 1895 with a chief designer named Mr A G Walters. Iridised tumblers found in Australia with the initials "AGW" were, initially, erroneously attributed to the "Australian Glass Works", where they actually related to Mr Walters! Apparently only tumblers were ever initialled, owing to production difficulties.

This Company was bought out in 1924/5 by the AGM Group and merged with another such amalgamation to become the Crown Crystal Glassworks and moved to a new address at Bourke Street, again in Waterloo, Sydney. Press ware manufacture continued from these premises.

Right top shows the logo of the Crown Crystal Glass works, whilst below it the picture depicts a sketch of the CHERUB design that follows the iridised intaglio-set DIANA and PANSY bowls.

Apparently the Australian buyers also delighted in the exported Sowerby (UK) range of iridised ware, advertised there under the description "Sunglo Range" and described in UK as "with Orange Flame Iridescence" (*Pottery Gazette* April 1931).

Manufacturing processes for Carnival Glass ware in the Australian Glasshouse have been described to the author by former workers. It appears that items such as Bowls, vases, flower frogs, compotes and fruit sets were all produced on a side-lever press. After being mould-pressed, each item was then placed in a "gloriole" and shaped to the desired style. Then it was deposited in a booth and, whilst still hot, was sprayed with a chosen solution of mainly Spirits of Salts and Chrome Oxide.

A temperature of 600°+F was sustained to ensure the successful adherence of the spray to the glass surface. This was a considerably higher temperature than was used in other producer countries, and maintained a lasting iridescence.

Patterns in Australian Carnival Glassware

The most well known patterns depict the local flora and fauna. We have *The Swan, Emu, Kookaburra, Shrike, Kangaroo, Kiwi, Crow, Kingfisher* and *Butterfly & Bower* bower. But these were complemented by other patterns less well-known overseas. There were the Swedish designs already mentioned as well as *Pin-Ups*, the *Heavy Diamond Float Bowl*, the elegant *Beaded Spears Water Set* (possibly from Sweden) as well as a *Parrots & Pomegranates Compote* and the *Birds & Cherries Bowl*. The latter two are shown in sketches left

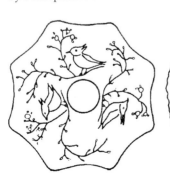

There is also a wide variety of Carnival Glass ware in Australia from both America and England, as well as the Swedish pieces that were

apparently iridised on the base for the Australian market, and arrived there via their UK Agents.

Design Registration for Australian Carnival Glass
Luckily, from the collector's point of view, many patterns in Australian Glassware were iridised and some Registrations appear on Carnival Glass manufactured there. There were Registered Numbers as well as Registered Designs (where the producer did not want his designs to carry a series of Registration Numbers – presumably for artistic reasons). Such registrations did not specify that the ware should be Carnival Glass and some of the Registrations were initiated prior to 1923 when iridised pressed ware was made.

A Kangaroo bowl has surfaced in moulded ware, in citron shade, but non iridised with an earlier Registration Number.

Several variations of design have appeared under the same Registration Number- whether because moulds were replaced and varied slightly, or whether there was a deliberate variation imposed, has not yet been established.

The following design Registrations have been reproduced from *Australian Glass of the Nineteenth and twentieth Century*, with kind permission of the author Mrs Marjorie Graham.

Reg No	Motif	Date applied for	Date published or period registered
4184	Kookaburra	4 Jan 1923	1 Apl-30 June 1923
4696	Kangaroo	15 Jan 1924	1 Oct-31 Dec 1924
4697	Swan	16 Jan 1924	1 Oct-31 Dec 1924
403600	Emu	14 Nov 1924	19 June 1925
40361	Kookaburra	14 Nov 1924	19 June 1925
40362	Lyre Bird	14 Nov 1924	27 Feb 1925
40363	Magpie	14 Nov 1924	27 Feb 1925
40364	Waratah	14 Nov 1924	13 Feb 1925
40547	Koala	8 Dec 1924	20 Feb 1925
44289	Kiwis	19 Apr 1926	13 Aug 1926

All except 44289 were originally applied for by Crystal Glass Ltd. The original applicant for KIWI motif was Crown Crystal Glass Co Ltd. The three numbers at the top of the list are Registered Designs and the corresponding number should be shown on the glassware. The remaining numbers are Registered Trade Marks. All marks and designs were first checked nationwide for possible infringements before granting applications.

Finally, we note here that there are two patterns quite difficult to find in Australian Carnival Glass Ware, namely:
(1) Eureka Floral Cross (Bowls) A set of one large and six small fruit bowls. Pattern *intaglio iridised* on the base exterior. The base glass is flint. The pattern shows a leafy cross motif with a stylised flower head at each point of the cross.
(2) Eureka Flag Fruit set. Here the cross is composed of dual straight lines (not leafy) and at each cross point there is a geometric star instead of a flower head.

Czechoslovakia

Modern political boundary changes have made the title Czechoslovakia obsolete, but we retain it for its general reference usage in the Carnival Glass world. Here we are strictly referring to the old Bohemia of Central Europe. This area sustained a tradition of glassmaking over many centuries and was the acknowledged leader in cut glass and art glass production throughout the European continent.

In Southern Bohemia a series of glassworks were founded in the latter part of the eighteenth century and these took up the desire for cheaper pressed ware as well as continuing with their crystal glass tradition when the markets changed in the 19th century.

Meanwhile in the North of the area, as early as 1836 the celebrated Joseph Lobmeyr turned to France to obtain new moulds, new machinery and a skilled workforce for the production of pressed glass. With this advent of mechanisation processes for manufacture in the mid 1800s, Bohemia also set up several Schools of Glassmaking so as to absorb the new techniques being introduced in America. By 1924 Bohemia was providing an extensive range of pressed and

Photograph taken between 1900 and World War II of the old and new furnaces at the J Riewdel complex at Unterpolaum (today called Desna). Here all the materials for use in the chain of glasshouses was produced. The old furnace was destroyed by fire in the 1950s.

coloured glassware for its European markets, as well as for export further afield. Prices were exceedingly low and the markets prospered and grew.

The Harrachov Glassworks, (founded in the North of Bohemia in 1712) became the major producer for the new pressed table and decorative ware. In 1887 the works was acquired by Joseph Riedel who came from a famous Bohemian Glassmaking family and he set about a massive expansion, ending up with a whole chain of Glasshouses. Riedel eventually became known as one of the greatest producers of luxury glass in his time. Export played a large role, to central Europe, to England and far beyond.

In England the *Pottery Gazette* of 1924 notes that a Mr Joseph Lohnert from Steinschonau and Gablonz in Bohemia was offering a wide range of crystal and coloured pressed glass for sale from his London showrooms. There was an attractive line of pressed coloured glass depicting Egyptian figures, intended to reflect the then current interest in the discoveries in the Valley of the Kings in Egypt.

Could this notice in the *Pottery Gazette* of 1924 refer to the the Classic Arts and Eqyptian Queen patterns, source unknown, that we collect nowadays from the early Carnival Glass production period? It has been established that the majority of the coloured and *iridised* pressed glass from Bohemia was intended for *export* rather than the home market. Items such as necklaces and handbags were also made using iridised pressed glass beads. A non-iridised bowl with this SAME pattern was also produced at Riihimaki, Finland!

Here are copies of various letterheads from correspondence with Riedel in 1902 by principal suppliers of minerals and materials for the glasshouses.

The Riedel Glassworks continues its tradition of producing fine art glass and domestic pressed tableware today, and exports worldwide. It is still renowned for quality of design and production. Modern style iridised pressed ware, in the form of lampshades, giftware etc is found worldwide.

England

Production of the English counterpart to the American Carnival Glass was a possibility considered by several English Glasshouses such as Davidson of Gateshead, Henry Greener works of Sunderland, H G Richardson of Stourbridge and the Sowerby works. Sowerby turned out to be the major contributor to such production.

Sowerby had set up business in 1765 but moved to its Ellison Glassworks in 1850. Here it rapidly became an established leader in the production of fine Art Glass as well as the more market orientated pressed glass tableware. So when, in 1911, the UK Trade Review *The Pottery Gazette* reported that the Fenton iridised pressed ware was selling extremely well in England, Sowerby was not slow to explore such a lucrative market circa the 1920s.

Sowerby iridised by spraying the glass whilst still hot with a variety of chemical solutions that were then 'sealed on' with refiring. This process resulted in the 'Sunglo' and 'Rainbo' range (ie marigold and blue and amethyst). Some earlier pressed glass designs such as Rowboat and Pinwheel have been found iridised. Sowerby was obviously keen to enter this field and used moulds to hand in the first instance.

Sowerby iridised pressed ware was marketed in direct competition with the various American producers ware. Fenton's range, described as being of 'Persian Gold' colour was selling through Fenton's local agent Mr C J Pratt of National Glass Company, Gamage Building, London. The Fenton USA green, blue and amethyst shades were the best sellers. Fenton also represented Imperial in England and an advertisement appears for the same in the Pottery Gazettes in 1911. Northwood ware was represented by Harry Northwood himself in 1908. The report of the death of his widowed mother Mrs John Northwood in 1908 (in the Pottery Gazettes) confirms this.

Sowerby responded with individualistic designs influenced by the Art Decoratif Movement, such as the "Swan covered butter" and "Hen covered butter", and with domestic table ware including stemmed and collar base sugars, milk jugs as well as various celery and salt shapes. A few items have also turned up in 'English Carnival Ware' that have been attributed to Davidson of Gateshead (such as Illinois Daisy Jar). But Sowerby soon developed into the major UK producer developing a vast production range of iridised as well as non-iridised pressed glassware.

The *Pottery Gazette's* of 1926 describe various Sowerby designs for sale, a boon for collectors where many of the Sowerby Catalogues were lost in Bombing raids during World War Two. Some still exist, so we can apply Catalogue Reference numbers in a few instances. A few (sadly incomplete) catalogue copies have even turned up at Eda Glassworks in Sweden, tucked away in the Production Manager's office!

Whilst the Sowerby designs were of quite individual and artistic form, few of the English pieces attained the high quality or the mass production numbers of their American counterparts or even of the Swedish ware being produced at Eda. Hand working was rare, and there was little green based glass. The majority of this ware was marigold. Even amethyst and blue are hard to find, and pastels practically non-existent apart from the odd aqua that has surfaced or the very rare Jet base glass. The latter two probably being of an experimental nature.

Some Sowerby carries the Peacock Head Trademark in the base and this is depicted in a small Pin Dish shown in this book under the pattern *Facets*. A sketch of the same, along with a drawing of the delightful *Covered Swan Butter* is shown left.

In the 1930s the iridised pressed glass line was re-vamped, new shapes appeared. The iridised bowls followed a 'squared-off' shape rather than the usual rounds or ovals. The bowl sides were straight and the glass was clear (flint). Many of the Sowerby iridised line pieces were obviously adapted from earlier moulds. So we find also the Wickerwork plate and its three legged stand in various *non iridised* colours such as opaque turquoise, opaque white (milk) and clear red, acid green, electric blue, and even a rather harsh pink.

At one stage, in an effort to avoid restrictive trade tariffs, Sowerby entered into business with Eda in Sweden. Patterns such as Wickerwork were actually *made* at Eda and despatched to UK for sale on wards to the Colonies through Sowerby. There is a letter in the Eda files where an English Agent refers to the *legal* requirement for origin labels on each piece, and wishes this were *not* the case!

Sowerby exported worldwide, particularly following the old Colonial trade routes to South Africa, India and Australia. Many pieces such as African Shield are also found in America and Marion Hartung found early examples of Lea and variant, Pineapple, Scroll Emboss and the Diving Dolphin Compote.

A 1915 *Pottery Gazette* notes a need for glass insulators. Apparently, during a survey of telegraph poles in a tropical rain forest, it had been noted that spiders sought shelter in the dark ceramic insulators and this caused the current to be deflected to the ground! Perhaps Sowerby read of this potential and made some Carnival Glass Insulators as well as its other designs so as to compete with the American versions!

Like other glasshouses, Sowerby was greatly affected by market forces worldwide and at home, and during the depression years suffered badly. By the 1970s this once great firm was reduced to making car windscreens – a sad reflection on its past glories. The works were demolished in 1982.

Estonia

The author has been able to establish proof of a limited production for iridised pressed ware in the 1930s at the Melesk Glasshouse in S Estonia. Unfortunately this factory burnt to the ground in 1992 and records were destroyed. However, local research instigated through private contacts and through the Museums in Estonia has elicited the following facts to date:

The Melesk Glassworks worked in close cooperation with their sister works at Riihimaki Finland. Many glass workers came to Estonia from Finland to assist in setting up a production scheme for producing iridised pressed glassware. In this book several patterns made at Melesk are noted as similar to those produced at Riihimaki – note the beautiful *Alexander Floral Water Set* (aka *Grand Thistle*) and the *Hobnail Banded Tumbler*. We also find patterns previously of unknown origins such as *Juliana, Stardust,* and *Starlight*.

Photograph from local archives showing the Melesk Glasshouse.

Local collectors and leading Museums in Estonia have meanwhile kindly given pieces for photography in this book, and research is continuing apace. It is probable that a considerable quantity of the production was for distribution throughout Russia.

Holland

Only one known producer of iridised pressed glassware circa 1920s has surfaced in this country to date. The author has established some production at the Royal Leerdam Works (now merged with the United Glassworks of Schiedam and operating as 'United Glassworks' (n.v.vereebigde glasfabrieken).

This glass blowing factory started way back in 1581 and as early as 1765 there was a bottle blowing plant at Leerdam. Clear and specially coloured household and decorative glassware as well as bottles was being produced by 1878.

In 1915 a Design School was established and prestigious architects K P C de Bazel, C de Lorm and C Lannoy headed the new venture. This proved very successful, so much so that other designers were signed up as well. By 1938 there was a SOLE designer, Mr Andrew Copier and in 1953 the predicate "Royal" was awarded to Leerdam Glass.. The Design School still flourishes and in the 1980s the Manager for the Design Team was Mr Floris Meydam. The *Meydam* pattern illustrated in this book is named after him, in recognition of his assistance with regard to identifying pieces made at Leerdam. There was *no* original pattern name given by Leerdam, items were just supplied with catalogue numbers.

PLAAT XXIX.
GEPERSTE MELKKANNEN. — CRÈMIERS MOULÉS.
MOULDED CREAMS.

No. 1935.   No. 2087.   No. 2127/no. 1.

No. 2127/no. 2.   No. 2171.   No. 2191.

Here is a copy of one of the Pages from the catalogue of the period covering pressed glass (and iridised pressed glass) production. There is no specific catalogue for iridised ware. Plate XX1X depicts various Creamer Jugs.

Carnival Glass collectors will no doubt recognise Catalogue Numbers 1935, 2087, 2127 (1 & 2) and there may well be the other creamers out there somewhere as export was important, particularly to the UK. The iridisation effect was particular to Leerdam, a mirror like surface often with a strong pink to the iridescence. This is referred to in the following from the UK *Pottery Gazette*:

Iridised wares of considerable artistic interest were also being produced at the Leerdam Glassworks in Holland. Some of these pieces, covered first with selenium and then having the surface iridised, were peculiarly brilliant to transmitted light.

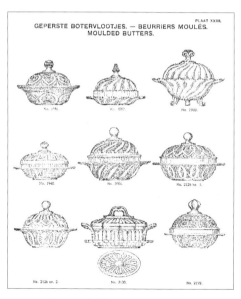

PLAAT XXVII.
GEPERSTE BOTERVLOOTJES. — BEURRIERS MOULÉS.
MOULDED BUTTERS.

No. 1781.   No. 1587.   No. 1933.

No. 1940.   No. 2066.   No. 2126 no. 1.

No. 2126 no. 2.   No. 2130.   No. 2192.

In the Butter Dish entries for the 1906 Leerdam Catalogue we can recognise such as *Beaded Swirl* and *Beaded Ovals*. It would appear that such items were only iridised to order. A *Punchbowl Set* look-alike to the American Imperial *Fashion* set was made at Leerdam and this is often found in the UK. This is shown on a slide in the archives at the National Glass Museum at Leerdam, stating manufacture circa 1910 at Leerdam!

Previous employees at Royal Leerdam confirm that production of iridised pressed ware was carried out as late as 1928 and shortly after, and that marigold, green. blue and amethyst base pressed ware was iridised to special order. The American Agents were Graham of New York (1906), Continuing production was noted in UK as late as 1931 (again in the trade gazette of the period).

Since the Dutch showed a marked liking for specific patterns namely Heart, Greek Key, Oakleaf and Acorn patterns, many puzzle pieces known will probably tie in with Dutch manufacture. The Greek Key and Sunburst Vase being one such possibility.

The fine detail in the designs presented by Leerdam were obviously intended to compensate for the fact that all the iridised pressed glass produced there was direct from the mould and there is no evidence of any hand-worked finish.

Scandinavia

For various historical, political and economic reasons, there had been a considerable upsurge in glass production in this area from the 1880,s. The mechanisation of the industry had proved a great impetus for expansion. Fine art glass traditions were continued along with a desire to enter and exploit both the pressed glass, and the iridised pressed glass, markets. New moulds were produced, new machinery in place and a skilled workforce was readily available.

Following after the American Glass houses, both Sweden and Finland were producers of their own iridised pressed ware, which they called Lustre Ware, although production was never major line. There appears to have been no production in Denmark or Norway. In Finland there were four glassfactories that made 'lustre ware', namely Iittala, Karhula, Kauklahti and Riihimaki. In Sweden, the Eda Glassworks was a major Scandinavian producer.

The Scandinavian designs all retained the detail for flowers or geometrics adopted by the American producers, but were quite distinctive in their own way both as regards production finishes, choice of design and colours of the base glass. Only a few pieces were adapted from the American patterns. These are shown right with sketches to illustrate.

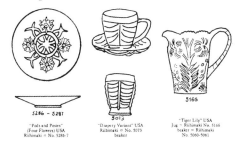

5286 – 5287
"Pods and Posies"
(Four Flowers) USA
Riihimaki = No. 5286-7

5073
"Diapery Variant" USA
Riihimaki = No. 5073
beaker

5166
"Tiger Lily" USA
Jug = Riihimaki No. 5166
beaker = Riihimaki
No. 5060-5061

To date,very few pieces have surfaced with animal designs. Roses and tulips are prolific in the field of floral design.

Production of the Scandinavian lustre ware took place between 1925 and the mid 1930s, though there was a short limited later production in the 1950s. The latter being easily recognised with more modern forms and design.

We now discuss the major Scandinavian producers in more detail.

Finland: Iittala Works

This was a minor producer and it is believed lustre ware may have been produced for the sister company at Karhula. Both were owned by the glassmaking consortium A Ahlstrom Oy factory. Iittala began glass production in 1881 and blown household glass, pressed glass cut crystal, engraved glass as well as bottles were all manufactured. Iittala still exists today, making blown household glass and light fittings, Export was considerable to other Scandinavian countries, and to Canada as well as to America.

There is a joint catalogue for Iittala works and Karhula works ware, this dated 1922. So far only **one** piece has been definitely attributed to Iittala. This is the pattern called *Quilted Fans*. It is catalogued as No 4800 Iittala.

Finland: Karhula Works

Karhula works was set up in 1888 and was renowned for fine art glass. From 1916 it was jointly owned with Karhula and Iittala Glasshouses by a private Company called A Ahlstrom Osakeyhtio and post 1941 took its own name as A. Ahlstrom Osakeyhtio Karhula.

At the beginning of the 1900s Karhula ware carried both name and pattern number (there was a 1902-10 Catalogue). But only catalogue numbers were in use during the 'Lustre Ware' production period which took place between the 1920s to 1930s. The author has given pattern names for Indexing purposes, with the original catalogue number where pertinent for pieces shown in this book.

It has been established through conversation with Master Blower Hugo Rask who was working at the factory in the 1926 period, that only pressed glassware was produced at Karhula during that period. Most of the work was of an experimental nature- new markets and new products were always the driving force behind such research. It is thought the lustre ware process appealed since it allowed the use of any molten glass that was slightly off the desired standard for quality or colour. The RIO glass (pink based) that was used at the works was extremely difficult to stabilise in production colour-wise. Lustre ware production was therefore limited in scope and since difficulties were encountered in controlling the iridisation process, such efforts were soon abandoned.

The catalogues make no mention of any specific *iridised* pressed ware – no doubts such pieces were taken from the pressed glass catalogue directly.

Some of the Karhula iridised pressed glass was however *shaped* after it came from the mould. It was subject to shaping at the end of a blow-pipe, and this was often applied to the manufacture of vases and some bowls. The press-moulds used were either in three or four sections.

Some catalogue entries are noted below. Such designs were not specifically original to Karhula since it operated closely with its sister Finnish glasshouses, exchanging work forces and designs. The Karhula Museum still retains some original moulds from the period.

Colour Formulae at Karhula

Base glass in use was either a light cobalt blue or 'antique rosa' (soft pink- named as **Rio** glass in the catalogues of the time).

An old book of Formulae has been found at the Karhula works that gives a clear insight into the manufacture of such glass.

There is a note to the effect that Karhula produced a slightly lighter blue than that in the Formula below (reducing the cobalt to 0.01 kg from the standard 0.3 kg as most probably in use at Kauklahti.)

Rio Glass		Dark Blue Glass	
Sand	130kg	Sand	130kg
Soda Ash	48kg	Soda Ash	55kg
Limestone	15kg	Baryta	2kg
Lead Minimum	6.5kg	Limestone	15lg
Saltpetre	5kg	Saltpetre	5kg
Borax	1.6kg	Arsenic	1kg
Arsenic	1kg	Feldspar	12kg
Iron Oxide	0.8kg	Cobalt	0.3kg
Sulphur Cadmium	0.8kg		
Selenium, Black	0.4kg		
Sulphur	0.1kg		
+ Lead Crystal Cullets	25kg		

All the manufacturers closely guarded their EXACT formulae for the metallic salts used in the chosen iridisation processes. At Karhula the Museum carried out a costly and detailed spectographic analysis on a dissolved lustre-layer on one of the pieces of lustre ware from Karhula. The results indicated an absence of all noble metals and also surprisingly, a lack of arsenic. The use of the latter had lead to the derivation of the term POISON GLASS as applied to Lustre ware in Estonia and in other areas of Scandinavian manufacture. But the following *were* found to be present:

Lead (100); Iron (2); Copper (1.5) and Chloride (1). The chloride is likely an indication of copper or iron oxide as a raw material in the mixture, the lead may be there as much as a binder than as a colourant.

Karhula Works used the German text book by Springer called *Die Glamakerei und Glasatzerei Insbesonders nach Ihr en Chemiseschen Grundlagen* (Zweisel 1923) when setting up its colour formulae for the iridisation process. The same source also notes the complications in producing lustre colours and recommends the purchase of already established lustre colours to save cost in production. Whether Karhula followed this advice is unknown. Since the glasshouse carried out their annealing process in ovens heated by generator gas, this would have permitted some control over any oxidisation process should the Company have decided to experiment with their own colours.

Springer's text relating to iridised ware, explains that the technique then available for obtaining a metal iridescence on glass with so-called 'lustre colours' differed from that previously described in the volume and that lustre colours were usually baked by means of an oxidisation fire without reduction. Thus obtained, such colour shades could not generally be modified by an altered atmosphere (i.e. by a reducing fire, not by increased temperature). It also stated that according to their composition lustre colours are organic metal compounds – so called resins and are soluble in volatile oils such as lavender oil etc. Many metals, apart from silver, copper and bismuth (rarely used) are freely employed. Such organic metal compounds are produced by either a dry method (dissolving the metal salt solution in colophony) or by a 'wet' method of separating the metal salt solution by the addition of a resinic acid metal, then treating it in various ways and finally dissolving it in oil.

The lustre colours themselves are either simple resinic acid metals with resinuous lead or bismuth added for better adhesion, or mixtures of resinic acid metals. Frequently phosphated or boracic compounds are used and leaf brass added.

This volume then goes on to give a list of some lustre colours as made up by R. Hohlbaum and these make interesting reading.

Iron lustre a reddish brown lustre consisting of 1 part resinous iron, 1 part resinous lead, 2 parts oil.
Cobalt lustre a grey lustre with little iridescence, consisting of 1 part resinous cobalt, 1 part resinous lead, 2 parts oil.
Mother of Pearl lustre 1 part resinous iron, 1 part resinous uranium, 2 parts resinous lead, 4 parts oil.
Pink Lustre pink lustre with gold reflections, 4 parts leaf brass, 1 part resinous lead, 4 parts oil.

The text then adds that lustre is applied either evenly, in stripes, or mottled onto the article by means of a brush. It is then baked in an oxidising fire. Only very occasionally (as in the case of silver lustre) does a reducing fire need to be used. The organic substances burn up in the muffle and a thin skin like layer of metal remains on the glass giving it a unique iridescent glitter in various metallic shades.

Whilst it is known that export was important to Karhula few records exist that detail such ventures as regards the lustre ware production lines, The glass photographed from Karhula in this book was all provided from the Museum of Glass at Karhula, with reference numbers as indicated.

Finland: Kauklahti
Between 1923 and 1952 there was a varied output from this factory, consisting of blown glass, pressed glass, cut crystal, engraved glass and bottles. The Company was owned by Riihimaki Lasi Oy (a private concern) between 1927-1952 and later specialised in its lampshade production ware. Between 1923-1927 it was in the ownership of one Claes Norstedt though there has been no indication of lustre ware production at this time.

Since Riihimaki Lasi Oy only produced pressed glass at its Kauklahti outlet between the 1920s and the 1930s, it would appear that the lustre ware was made in the 1930s when the ownership had passed from Norstedt. Although owned by Riihimaki the factory retained its individuality as a manufacturing Company till as late as 1941.

The designs for this Company follow those of Riihimaki and there is no separate catalogue. But according to local sources, the pattern named **Fircones** from Riihimaki (a pitcher and tumbler set) was also made at the Kauklahti works.

Finland: Riihimaki
This factory was set up in Southern Finland in 1910 and still exists as a major concern to this day. Now it is a fully automated bottle plant, though it has a fine history of production of blown household glass, pressed glass, cut crystal, engraved glass as well as bottles.

Translation from Swedish
News! News!

The ultramodern Lustra-Hoh'to glass products not previously which glitter in a most wonderful symphony of colour are the latest novelty from the Riihimaki glass factory to attract attention.

By choosing Lustra-Hoh'to glasses in just the shades which are in harmony with other colours of the room you can make each and every glass item further enhance the general effect of the room or table service.

Riihimaki's ingenious manufacturing methods have enabled exceedingly low prices.

Take Lustra-Hoh'to glasses into consideration – they are a pleasure for the eye. Most of the shops which sell glass will also sell Lustra-Hoh'to glass.

O. Y. RIIHIMÄKI

Translation from Finnish

The astoundingly beautiful Hoh'to-Lustra glass products not previously seen here which glitter in a most wondrous symphony of colour are the most recent novelty from the Riihimaki glass factory to attract attention.

By selecting just those Hoh'to-Lustra glasses which have the right shades of colour to match the other colours of the room you will be able to make each glass item enhance the general effect of the room or the table service.

Riihimaki's ingenious manufacturing methods have made it possible to sell these new products at exceedingly lwo prices.

You should go to take a look at Hoh'to-Lustra glasses. Most shops selling glass products will also sell Hoh'to-Lustra glasses.

O. Y. RIIHIMÄKI

Advertisements for iridised pressed glassware from Riihimaki.

It is believed that production of lustre ware did not take place till the 1930s. There is mention of lustre ware in a Riihimaki Catalogue of the era, relating to an iridised ashtray. We also have the advert (above) as released by Riihimaki in the early 1930s – it is in both Swedish and Finnish.

The Riihimaki outlet also produced a brief later range of iridised pressed glass as we know from the catalogues in existence between 1954 and 1957. This was mainly for export and sold well in America. But it is understood that only the **Rio** base-colour glass (pink) was made at this time. All blue-based glass was from the earlier period. Like its sister factories, only **Rio** or **Blue** lustre ware appears to have been made in the 1930' s period in Finland, though some one-off pieces in amethyst might be possible.

Riihimaki adopted two known methods for producing iridised pressed glassware:

1. The object to be iridised was painted with metal oxide and fired at about 500°C (the same temperature as used in Australian production).

2. The object was held in metal oxide steam and fired in a dce-oxidising (reducing) flame so that the oxide de-oxidised into an iridised surface.

The steam was poisonous and in Finland the glass often bore the unfortunate designation of 'Poison Glass' since, in the second process noted, the mass of glass retained in it the same oxides as the steam (whereby the composition of iridised glass thus differs from that of ordinary pressed glass). Furthermore there was always the dangerous lead content to contend with.

Bismuth, silver, copper, platinum, gold and antimony were used in this process of iridisation. Both Riihimaki and Kauklahti used the second, and poisonous, method of iridisation, which was not employed at Karhula works.

At Riihimaki it was also understood that the Russians used a third method of iridisation whereby a very thin sheet of metal (1/1000 width) was employed.

At Riihimaki a vast quantity of the lustre ware production was exported to Russia, as well as to Europe and Scandinavia.

With regard to designs, it is interesting to note the similarity between some American and Riihimaki designs. Designs from the Riihimaki catalogues, show remarkable similarities with American patterns <u>Tiger Lily</u> (Imperial), <u>Drapery</u> Variant (Northwood), and <u>Four Flowers</u> (Northwood).

Sweden : EDA (1830-1953)

Eda Glasbruk (Eda Glass Manufacturing Co) was established close to Charlottenberg on the Norwegian/ Swedish border in SW Sweden in 1830. Up until closure Eda manufactured all kinds of glass, from greenish windowpanes and bottles to deep cut crystal bowls and wineglasses, as well as the unique honey-coloured and palest blue pieces made in the modern Scandinavian style. There was even thin-blown glass in the Venetian tradition.

Pressed glass also formed an important part of the production at Eda, from the first salts and tumblers made in 1845, then plates and candlesticks in the 1890s, and thereafter all sorts of bowls, vases and tumblers in various colours up till 1953. In the earlier days, at the turn of the century, Eda was one of the three most important glasshouses in Sweden, employing 300 men and managing an off-shoot sister company with a new factory at Magnor Norway. The majority of the glass then produced at Eda (around 75%) was sold within Norway but there was some export to England, the USA, Canada and Australia.

Drawing of the Eda Catalogue frontispiece of 1929.

Throughout the period 1909-31 the pressed glass output consisted of more than 50% of the total Eda production and an attempt to export was made. Domestic items such as sugar bowls, creamers, fruit bowls, match holders and simple tumblers were all on offer.

The Eda factory closed down for a few years after 1933, as following the period covering iridised pressed glass production, the markets were heavily depressed. But just prior to this period (1927-33) a new modern 'Scandinavian Design' concept was introduced and production changed from cheap oppressed glass products to an exclusive and hand made style of crystal ware. Such pieces were either thin blown and lightly coloured, or heavier weight bowls mainly in a panel design on soft honey, pale gray, a delicate light blue or a soft caramel brown. Such designs were the work of Gerda Stromberg who was married to the Eda Glass Company Manager Edward Stromberg. Some pieces from this period can be found in the Victoria and Albert Museum in England.

Eda Glassware was first introduced onto the UK market by agents R Johnston and later by Jules Wuidart, Bowman and Son, as well as Elfversson all of London, and Doleman and Steward in Glasgow. Here is a letter from a director at R Johnston.

At one time R Johnston held the sole selling rights for

Eda in Australia though there is also evidence of direct orders from the Aurora Glass Company, of Richmond Melbourne as well as from Melbourne Reindorffs of Brisbane. On the American market Eda was represented by J H Venon (New York) as well as by George Borgfelst & Co (New York USA and Toronto Canada).

Eda Lustre Ware Production

A few records exist concerning iridisation on **blown** glass both from Eda and from the sister factory at

Photograph of the Workers at Eda at the time of iridised lustre ware production.

Magnor in Norway. These relate to the start of the twentieth century. The production of **Iridised Pressed Ware** (ie Lustre ware / Carnival Glass) started early in 1925 and went on for some years. Production ceased when the factory closed temporarily in 1933 (in the Recession) and **iridised**

pressed glass was never made again when the factory opened its doors again between 1935-1940 and 1943-1953.

The traditional belief in the Eda area is that the Carnival Glass (as we call it) was introduced by the old Executive Leader, one Gustav Kessmeier and that he alone held the secret production formula for the iridisation. This he had apparently obtained from his son Arthur who worked for an American glass company!. Mr Kessmeier supervised the iridisation process himself on a daily basis, arriving with a small bottle dangling from a cord around his waist, the contents of which were used to control the iridisation process.

Production reached as high as 900 pieces per day before the Great Depression. Then sales dropped radically and stocks were left in barrel-loads in local unlocked warehouses – it was realised no-one would bother to steal such an apparently unsaleable product.

The local population was totally involved in the works – there was a strong Temperance Club Movement and in 1920 a group of workers from Eda went to work at Corning USA and formed The Swedish Band there. The two photographs right show these groups.

Top: Members of the Temperance Club movement at Eda in 1920.
Bottom: The Swedish Eda Factory Band in the 1920s.

The export of Lustre Ware from Eda

A few records exist concerning export in which Iceland as well as Norway were noted. We have already made reference to business with Australia and England. Possible export to Russia (as was carried out from the Finnish Glasshouses) has not been established. Agents records from abroad are not particularly detailed, pressed glass often included iridised pressed glass. But with the UK sales it has been found that certain agents took on the exclusive use of one design each from Eda. The patterns BERLIN and TOKYO were made in iridised form and were included in these agreements.

A letter (right) from one of the UK Agents, namely Doleman and Steward of Glasgow is reproduced here.

The presses, moulds and handling of lustre ware production

Presses and moulds were obtained from several places in Sweden, Germany, the UK and USA. Many of the moulds made for Eda were from Germany via Wilhelm Kutzscher of Deubner Glasformenfabrik, Dresden. Here is a letter from the Company.

Since there was a surplus of glass producers in Scandinavia (as elsewhere worldwide) during the Great Depression, many were forced into closure. Eda was thus able to buy-out many moulds from these other factories. Likewise, when Eda was forced to close in 1933 many of these moulds were then sold off to other Swedish factories and to Magnor in Norway and some to Karhula in Finland. It was Nils Hansson, the Executive Leader at Eda who moved on to work at Karhula who probably arranged for some of the sales from Eda to his new place of work. It is not know however whether these moulds, once sold, were ever again used for lustre ware production.

Many of the moulds are still stored at Magnor and the photographs shown below depict those involved in lustre ware production at Eda.

Right top: YORK pattern mould still at Magnor, Norway.
Below: A piece of machinery as used at the Magnor factory.
Right bottom: The FLEUR DE LIS mould now on show at Magnor, Norway originally from Eda works. This is also a well-known pattern in American production.

Base glass colours used at Eda during the lustre ware production

Base glass colouring was an old tradition at Eda, starting with a strong blue base, and with brown and soft yellow base shades. There was also some limited production on opaque white (blanc-de lait / milk glass) and also on dark amethyst and jet. The latter was NOT black amethyst but actual jet glass. These base colours were introduced in the manufacture of chemists bottles as early as 1850.

A series of new colours followed from 1880 till 1900 and these were light green opaque (called 'mallakitt' – malachite), along with several shades of blue and green, and even a version of the popular English Cranbery Red. During WW1 and after there was another set of colours introduced, mostly in soft 'juice' colours such as soft raspberry, soft apricot etc. A very few pieces of iridised ware appear on a soft blue background with heavy marigold overlay. There are a few and exceedingly rare pieces on blanc-de -lait with a clear iridescence over. A single RED base glass has been found iridised as a Bonbonniere lid in the **Lagerkrantz** pattern.

Some Eda ware has been found on pale lavender base, soft yellow base, pale pink (RIO) base, and even soft green or jet. But these are obviously one-off production and much sought after. Since Eda used its base glass colours indiscriminately for blown or pressed ware, this explains how the odd iridised pieces turn up in unusual base-glass shades as well.

Mould Designs

Designs were intricate and elaborate, well executed. Roses and CURVED STAR patterns (the latter imported and extended upon from Imperial USA) were much favoured. But many designs were also original to Eda. The two drawings on the right depict such patterns that appear only to emanate from Eda.

The quality of Eda lustre ware

Eda 'Carnival Glass' is of exceptional quality. A good base-glass is used in most cases, with a controlled iridescence over, often deep gunmetal in colour. There is superb mould work and the collar bases are ground-off by fine stone-cutting.

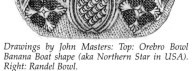

Drawings by John Masters: Top: Orebro Bowl Banana Boat shape (aka Northern Star in USA). Right: Randel Bowl.

Many Swedish collectors believe it is possible to identify an Eda lustre ware piece by the STAR pattern appearing on the base of the ware. But this is not wholly accurate since there are various star base patterns at Eda, some *not* in the catalogues. But there may well be a basis for this idea since the Kutzscher mould production firm in Dresden that supplied Eda with some of its moulds often favoured various star designs in the base of their moulds. This is notified in the advertising text as 'stern in boden' ie 'star in base'.

The tradition for so decorating the base of pressed glassware probably derived from that of working expensive blown and cut glass,where it was sought to conceal the pontil mark by an elaborate cut star. When we look at specific patterns from Eda, such as **Tokio** for example, we find a unique base design: a stylised version of the old Indo-European symbol for the sun- later reversed to form what we call a Swastika. This is an extremely rare piece to find from Eda and fetches a high price even where the base glass is standard deep blue.

Some of the Eda floral patterns have base patterns as well, some have a traditional star. some are left plain. Some Eda lustre ware was also hand-worked after leaving the mould, but again such pieces are hard to find.

Picture (right) shows a catalogue excerpt for the NANNA pattern range (mis-named by the advertiser as NANNY in this instance). and the next page shows three original blueprints from Eda: (i) the magnificent Rosor Vase (which is found in two sizes); (ii) Diamont Bonbonniere and (iii) Edstrom Plate. The Rosor Vase is also found on non-iridised red base glass in both sizes.

The Eda lustre ware production took place in 1927 when the Great Depression occurred. A short time after a new Managing Director was called in, by name Edward Stromberg and he set about returning to the production of expensive blown art glass instead of pressed glass. The press teams were reduced from eight to two in a very short while and lustre ware from Eda was never a proposition from that moment on.

PRÅSSGLASMÖNSTER "NANNY"　　Tillverkas vid EDA GLASBRUK

Left: Roser blueprint. Right: Diamant Bonbonniere blueprint. Below: Edstrom plate.

We end this chapter on a personal note! Immediately below we show a drawing of Eda (now in postcard format), drawn by Sven Morfeldt (1991 postcard).

Next follows an early photograph of the same Sven Morfeldt relaxing in front of his bicycle, reading a local journal. This was taken during the Eda Lustre Ware production era.

For interested collectors it is worth noting that Magnor Glassworks in Norway ahs a superb Glass Museum relating to both Magnor and Eda glass making through the ages. There is also a fine retail sales outlet for current glass ware production.

At Karlstad in Sweden there is also a most interesting display of Eda pressed glassware (iridised and non-iridised). Efforts are currently underway to try and rescue the old Eda Glassworks Production site and bring it into public display.

Finally, we show two photographs, side by side. The author can be seen in the first, researching with local Eda Glass collectors at Eda. In the second, we see Gunnar Lersjo (glass photographer for the majority of the ware shown in this book). He is taking a photograph of a piece of Eda pressed 'lustre ware' at an Eda Collectors' Club meeting.

Photographic and Drawings Guide

This guide follows three sequences:
Single shots – In alphabetical sequence of pattern name
Group shots – All pieces identified by pattern name
Single drawings – in alphabetical sequence of pattern name

All patterns depicted throughout are to be found (with appropriate page reference) under the combined alphabetical pattern name index and price guide.

Pattern Name sources
Established Marion Hartung (USA) nomenclature
or
as named by production source.
Where named by the author, in italics.

Photographic sources
Photography by Gunnar Lersjo (Sweden) unless otherwise noted by:
**Howard Seufer (USA) for Fenton Glassware;
***Courtesy Museum of Applied Arts and Sciences, Sydney, Australia,
or source as noted.

Abbreviations used relating to production sources

AUS	Australia	FRI	Finland: Riihimaki
BSL	Belgium: Val St Lambert	HRL	Holland: Royal Leerdam
CZA	Czechoslovakia	SWE	Sweden: Eda
ENG	England: manufacturer unknown	USD	USA: Duggan
ESB	England: Sowerby	USDD	USA: Dugan/Diamond
EMK	Estonia: Melesk	USF	USA: Fenton
EUR	European: manufacturer unknown	USI	USA: Imperial
FII	Finland: Iittala	USM	USA: Millersburg
FDK	Finland: Karhula	USN	USA: Northwood
FDI	Finland: Kauklahti	n/k	not known

NB Not all Scandinavian Source names relate SOLELY to pattern. They CAN relate to particular shapes. Thus a bowl or pitcher in the SAME pattern might well bear DIFFERENT NAMES. Be aware!

*Where possible accepted American pattern names have been used, (depicted in **bold italics**) but some producer countries did not name their ware, or all of their iridised ware. In such cases the author has suggested temporary titles indicative of pattern style only, and these are depicted in italics.*

ACANTHUS (USI) plate, Smoke, £125/$125.

ACORN (USF) bowl, Blue, £90/$90.

ACORN BURRS (USN)** punch bowl top and base, Marigold, bowl set £350/$350, punch cup £25/$25. Ex-Fenton Art Glass Museum.

(AUTUMN) ACORN (USF) bowl, 8", worked candy edge add 25%, Blue, £95/$95.

AFRICAN SHIELD (ESB) mustard or jam jar and lid (metal with hole for spoon), Marigold on Clear, £40/$40.

ALEXANDER FLORAL (FRI) Blue Pitcher £1700/$3060 and Tumbler £300/$540.

AMERIKA (SWE). Stubby footed small bowl. Extremely rare Milk Glass, iridised Clear, £900/$1620.

APPLE BLOSSOM TWIGS (USDD)** bowl, circa 1910-15, Amethyst, rare in UK, £250/$250. Ex Fenton Art Glass Museum, USA.

APPLE PANELS (USD) panelled sugar, Marigold, £30/$30.

ARCS (USI) external pattern to Star of David bowl. £180/$180.

ARGYLE (HRL) stemmed cake plate, Marigold in Royal Leerdam Catalogue. £65/$115.

ASTRID (SWE) bowl, Marigold £85/$155.

ATHENA (SWE) bowl (shallow), Marigold on Blue, £85/$155.

AUSTRALIAN CRYSTAL CUT (AUS) compote, Black Amethyst, £250/450.

AUSTRALIAN PANELS (AUS). Crown Crystal Glassworks, two-handled sugar, Black Amethyst, £165/$300.

BASKETWEAVE (USN) bowl, Green, exterior to Wishbone with worked edge.

BEADED BASKET (USD) two-handled, Amethyst, £55/$55.

BEADED CABLE (USN) candy dish, footed, Amethyst, exterior pattern, £85/$85.

BEADED SPEARS (AUS) Crown Crystal Glass, tumbler, Marigold on Clear £120/$215. Pitcher at £360/$650.

BEADED CRYSTAL AND RAYS (EUR) small bowl, Marigold on Clear £20/$35.

BEARDED BERRY (USF) (exterior to and see PEACOCK AND URN) on Aqua Base, a one-off bowl £3000/$3000.

BEADS AND DIAMONDS (HRL) butter dish base only, ex-Royal Leerdam Pressed Glass Catalogue, with lid. £000/$000

BEARDED BERRY (USF)**. Exterior to and see PETER RABBIT bowl. Ex- Fenton Art Glass Museum USA.

BEAUTY BUD (USD) vase, Marigold on Clear, £65/$65.

BELL AND ARCHES (USD) *deep bowl, Marigold on Clear, £38/$38. Scarce in UK.*

(FROLICKING) BEARS *Spittoon. International Carnival Glass Association Souvenir (ICGA), Elkhart 1982, as noted on piece, £85/$155. Shown with ICGA TOWN PUMP Souvenir. Originally a USG Pattern.*

BEAUTY BUD TWIG (USD) *vase, very rare in miniature, Amethyst, £835/$835.*

BERLIN (SWE) *bowl, named ex-Eda Catalogue, £235/$425.*

BIRD WITH GRAPES *wall vase, manufacturer not known. Marigold on Clear, Large wall vase, £75/$135. Scarce in UK.*

BIRDS AND CHERRIES (USF)** *bowl, Blue, £/$n/k. Ex-Fenton Art Glass Museum USA.*

SINGING BIRDS (USN) *tumbler. Rare Ice Green, £300/$300, and see PASTEL SWAN (USD/USF).*

(WILD) BLACKBERRY (USF) *bowl with crimped edge, Green £185/$185.*

BLACKBERRY (USN) *compote on three legs, Amethyst, £75/$75.*

BLACKBERRY BLOCK (USF)** *water set, Marigold, pitcher £400+/$400, tumbler £48/$48+. Ex-Fenton Art Glass Museum USA.*

BLUEBERRY (USF)** *water set, Marigold, pitcher £400/$400, tumbler £85/$85. Ex-Fenton Art Glass Museum USA.*

Bo–Bu

BORDERED PENDANT (FDK) tumbler. Catalogue No 4016, Blue £350/$630, extremely rare. Four section mould. Courtesy Karhula Lasimuseo.

BROKEN ARCHES (USI) punch bowl and cups, bowl top and base £180/$335. Cups each £25/$45.

BUTTERFLIES (USF) Bon-Bon, two-handled, Green, £55/$55.

BUTTERFLY AND TULIP (USD)**. Master bowl, interior pattern. Amethyst £3000/$3000+. Ex-Fenton Art Glass Museum.

BOUQUET (USF)** water set, Blue, pitcher £650/$650, tumbler £70/$70. Ex-Fenton Art Glass Museum USA.

BROOKLYN BRIDGE (USD) bowl, Marigold, £140/$140. Unlettered version at £800/$800.

BUTTERFLY AND BELLS (AUS) compote, profile view, Black Amethyst, $£240/$430.

BUTTERFLY AND TULIP (USD)** Master bowl, exterior pattern Amethyst, £3000/$3000+. Ex-Fenton Art Glass Museum.

BOWMAN (SWE) bowl, Marigold, £85/$155. Similar to NUTMEG grater Sowerby UK. Named at factory source.

BULLS EYE AND LEAVES (USN). Exterior pattern to bowl, Green, £35/$35.

BUTTERFLY AND BERRY (USF) knob footed bowl, 10", Green, £185/$185.

BUTTERFLY AND BOWER (AUS)***. Crown Crystal Glass-works Deep bowl, Marigold, with BROKEN CHAIN exterior, £180/$335.

BUTTON AND HOB (ESB) bowl, Blue (rare base colour) £85/$155.

CANDLESTICKS (Obsidian) on rare Jet base glass. Origin not known, £260/$470 Pair.

CAR VASE, manufacturer not known, Marigold on Clear, £35/$65.

CHARLIE (SWE) large bowl, Blue base, £265/$480.

CHERRY (USM) sugar and creamer set, Green, £135/$135 Set.

CHERRY (USM)** milk pitcher, Green, circa 1910, £1200/$1200 (approx). Extremely rare. Ex-Fenton Art Glass Museum.

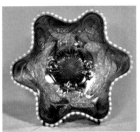

CHERRY (USD) bowl, 8", Peach Opalescent, £165/$165.

CHERRY (USD) bowl, on three legs, Red (dark), £650/$650.

CHERRIES AND BLOSSOM (USF)** water set, Blue, pitcher £380/$380, tumbler £135/$135. Ex-Fenton Art Glass Museum.

(ENAMELLED) CHERRIES (USF) tumbler, Blue, £135/$135.

CHRYSANTHEMUM (USF) Master bowl on three curl-toed legs, Blue, £285/$285.

CHERRY CHAIN (USF) bowl, 6", Red, £450/$450.

Right: CHUNKY (ESB) bowl, Blue (rare colour) £60/$110.

CHUNKY (ESW) two-tier fruit bowl with central metal handle, £90/$160.

CLASSIC ARTS (CZA/FRI) rose bowl, Marigold. Seen in Riihimaki Finland Glass Museum. Very hard to find in UK £325/$585.

CLEVELAND (USM) commemorative memorial tray, Amethyst. Not available in UK to date, $11000.

COBBLESTONES (USI) bowl, Amethyst, 8", £90/$90.

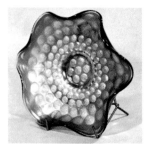

COIN DOT (USF) bowl, Marigold iridescent on Aqua base (extremely rare), £20/$20.

CONCORD LATTICE (USF)** bowl, Green, Fenton Cat No 1036, 1911. Hand-worked edge £360/$360. Personally chosen by Mr Frank Fenton for inclusion in this book. Ex-Fenton Art Glass Museum USA.

COOKIE (USI) plate with central handle, Smoke, £185/$185.

COVERED HEN (ESB). Very rare butter and lid, Blue, £300/$540.

CORN VASE souvenir, HOACGA (USA). Ice Blue, 6"+, £78/$78.

COSMOS AND CANE, US Glass, (USA) bowl (small), 5", Marigold. Similar design adapted in Finland.

COVERED SWAN (ESB). Rare butter and lid, Marigold, £135/$245. Note intricacy of Swan neck moulding.

CRACKLE (USI) water set, Marigold on Clear, pitcher £90/$90, tumbler £30/$30.

CROW (AUS) bowl on Black Amethyst, £250/$450.

CROW (AUS) bowl (small), on Black Amethyst, £250/$450.

DAISY AND PLUME (USN/ USDD). Exterior pattern to BLACKBERRY.

CRACKLE (USI/Scandinavia). Single Epergne in metal stand, Marigold on Clear, £85/$85.

CUT ARCHES (FRI) Banana Boat Shape, £85/$155 excellent iridescence.

DAGNY (SWE) vase, part of Curved Star range, Blue, Rare £385/$695.

DAISY SPRAY (SWE) vase with flared or turned-in top, Blue, £365/$660.

CROSS HATCH (EUR) stemmed sugar bowl, Marigold, £35/$65. Possibly Sowerby UK.

CYNTHIA (ESB) vases with turned in tops, extremely rare Jet glass. Part of Sowerby Derby Range, Art Deco Style, £850/$1550 each. There is also a taller centre console vase with flared lip. Pair matching £2000/$3600.

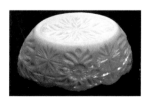

DAINTY goblet Indiana (USA) reproduction goblet, blue base, £48/$48.

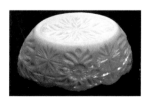

DAISY SPRAY (SWE), shallow straight sided bowl, clear iridescence on Milk glass. Extremely rare in colour and quantity, £800/$1440.

De–Di

DECORATED CARNIVAL No 1 (USF)** water set on Blue. Cat No 1014, 1910. Value not known. Ex-Fenton Art Glass Museum.

DECORATED CARNIVAL No 2 (USF)** water set on Blue, circa 1910. Value not known. Ex-Fenton Art Glass Museum.

DIAMANT (SWE) Bonbonniere and lid, Blue, only one known. £850/$1550.

DIAMONDS (USM) water set, Amethyst, pitcher £380/$380, tumbler £120/$120.

DIAMOND & WEDGES (SWE) bowl (large), Blue, £225/$405.

DIAMOND DAZZLER, (EUR) stubby pitcher, high sheen. No tumblers seen to date. May be English as similar to FANS water set (English).

DIAMOND LACE (USI) bowl (small), 5", Amethyst, £60/$60.

STIPPLED DIAMOND SWAG, (EUR) compote on stem, Marigold, £000/$000.

HEAVY DIAMONDS (AUS) float bowl and Central Flower Frog, Black Amethyst, £285/$515.

MITRED DIAMONDS AND PLEATS (ESB). Two-handled small pin dish, often found with Sowerby Peacock Head Trademark, Marigold on Clear, £28/$50.

DIAMOND PRISMS, (EUR/USA?) compote on stem, Amber base £65/$115.

DIANA (SWE/AUS) bowl. Crystal with Intaglio iridised base pattern, £165/$300. Probably sent to Australia for iridisation ex-Sweden.

DIVING DOLPHINS (ESW) bowl
on elaborate legs, Amethyst,
£260+/\$470, with flared top, in
Amethyst, £000/\$000; with squared
off sides, Amethyst, \$310/\$000.

DIVING DOLPHINS (ESW) bowl
as left internal scroll embossed
pattern shown.

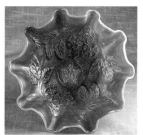

DOGWOOD SPRAYS (USD)
compote, crimped, domed base, Peach
Opalescent, £300/\$300.

DRAGON AND STRAWBERRY
(USF) bowl, Marigold, £300/\$300.
Rare in UK.

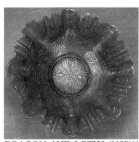

DRAGON AND LOTUS (USF)**
bowl as Butler Bros Catalogue 1913,
on rare Topaz Base, £165/\$165
(estimate). Ex-Fenton Art Glass
Museum USA.

DRAGON AND LOTUS (USF)**
bowl on rare Red base. Fenton Cat No
1656, £4000+/\$4000. Ex-Fenton Art
Glass Museum .

DRAGON'S TONGUES (USF)
electric light shade, Marigold on
Milk. Cat No 230 Circa 1914,
£165/\$165.

DRAPERY (USN) rose bowl, small
Amethyst, £95/\$95.

DREIBUS (USN)** advertising
dish. Small bowl, one side up, turned
hand grip Amethyst, £500+/\$500.
Ex-Fenton Art Glass Museum.

EDSTROM (SWE). Banana Boat
shape bowl, Blue, £425/\$765. Ex-Eda
Cat No 2411, 1929.

EGG AND DART (EUR)
Depression Ware stubby candlestick,
reverse fruit dish, £15/\$25.

(ATLANTIC CITY) ELK (USF)**
shallow bowl. Blue, very rare,
£900/\$900. Ex-Fenton Art Glass
Museum.

(TWO EYED) ELK *(USM) bowl, Amethyst, 1910, £625/$625.*

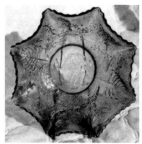

EMU *(AUS)*** bowl on rare Aqua base, £380/$685.*

EMU *(AUS)*** compote, Marigold on clear, £360/$650.*

ENAMELLED CLEMATIS *(CZA?) wine set, decanter and goblets partially iridised and decorated. £850/$1550 set.*

ENGLISH HOBSTAR *(EUR) Marigold oval bowl set in metal basket holder, £85/$155 with holder; £35/$65 without holder. This is also a Finnish pattern.*

FAN *(USD) sauce boat in Peach Opalescent, £165/$165.*

FANLIGHT, *possibly Val St Lambert Belgium. Double two-pronged candlestick, also seen in Pale Green in Belgium, £95/$170.*

FACETS *(ENG) large fruit bowl with 6 smaller bowls on curled toe legs. Marigold on Clear £85/$155 Set.*

FANS *(ENG) water set, Marigold on clear, excellent iridescence, only known English water set to date. Pitcher and six tumblers, £180/$335 (pitcher available in 2 sizes).*

FANTAIL *(USF)**. Three-toed bowl, Blue, £185/$185. No 1126. Ex-Fenton Art Glass Museum.*

FARMYARD *(USDD)** bowl, Amethyst, interior pattern shown, £5000+/$5000. One of the rarest and most sought after USA patterns. Ex-Fenton Art Glass Museum.*

FEATHER AND HEART *(USM)** water pitcher. Green, circa 1910, £800+/$800. Ex-Fenton Art Glass Museum.*

FENTONIA *(USF)** water set. Blue, Pitcher £700/$700, tumbler £200/$200. Ex-Fenton Art Glass Museum.*

FERN *(USN) compote on fine stem, Green, £75/$75.*

FILE *(USI) bowl (small), Amethyst, exterior pattern, £45/$45.*

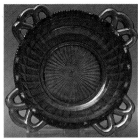

FILE *(ESB) small Sowerby Nappy with exterior FILE pattern. Marigold on Clear. With Trademark Head £28/$50.*

FINE CUT OVALS *(USM)** bowl. Green, exterior pattern here to WHIRLING LEAVES, £220/$220. Ex-Fenton Art Glass Museum.*

FINE CUT RINGS, *(UK) made for Guggenheim in 1925. Celery vase, Marigold on Clear, often with Registration Mark, £65/$115. Shown here with fine band vase.*

FIRCONES *(FRI) water set. Blue, pitcher £1200/$2160, tumbler £350/$630. Limited production, rare. Riihimaki Model No 5161. Possibly also made at FDI, Finland.*

FIR CONE *(USF) (aka PINE CONE) bowl, 5", Amethyst, £65/$65.*

FISH BOWL *(EUR) shallow bowl with straight sides, Intaglio Fish in base. Iridised all over bowl £38/$70. Also seen Fish only iridised.*

(LITTLE) FISHES *(USF) bowl (small), on three legs, Blue, £225/$225.*

FLORAL AND GRAPE *(USF)** water set variant, on Blue, pitcher £285/$285, tumbler $98/$98. Ex-Fenton Art Glass Museum. Note: number of petals in daisies/direction of ribs in band.*

(ENAMELLED) FLOWERS (USF)
bowl (small), Marigold, £85/$85.

(FOUR) FLOWERS (SWE/FRI?)
bowl with THUMBPRINTS exterior
and Flowers between Crab Claws on
rare Pastel Yellow base £650/$1170.

(FOUR) FLOWERS (SWE). This
version in Pastel Blue ultra thin glass
with worked-edge. No Thumbprints
exterior. No flowers between crab
claws. Marigold iridescence.
Extremely rare version £550/$990.

(FOUR) FLOWERS (USD) small
shallow bowl on Peach Opalescent
Base. No pattern on exterior and no
Flowers between Crab Claws. Fairly
easy to find in USA, £125/$125.

(FOUR) FLOWERS (USA/Scand.
versions). This version, Eda Sweden.
Shallow bowl cum plate, Emerald
Green base glass, £265/$265.
THUMBPRINTS exterior and
flowers between crab claws.

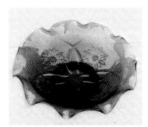

(FOUR) FLOWERS (SWE) bowl,
worked edge on thin Lavender Pastel
Base. No exterior pattern, no fruit
between crab claws. Rare in this form
and colour £550/$990.

(LITTLE) FLOWERS (USF) bowl,
9", Marigold, £75/$75.

(TWO) FLOWERS (USF) bowl on
spatula feet, Green, £68/$68.

FOOTED PRISMS (ESB) vase,
pedestal base, Blue, £325/$585.

FLOWERS AND FRAMES
(USDD) bowl (shallow), Amethyst,
£200/$200.

Left: FORMAL FLOWERS creamer,
origin not known, Marigold on Clear,
£35/$65.

FOUR-SEVEN-FOUR (USI) pitcher, Marigold on Clear, £180/$180.

FOUR SIDED TREE TRUNK vase (EUR), Marigold on Clear, £88/$160.

FREEHAND (ENG?). A solid glass handshape with Purple iridisation over on Deep Blue glass. Possibly Modern, £84/$155.

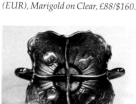

(TWO) FRUITS (USF). Two-sided split dish, Amethyst, £95/$95.

FROSTED BLOCK (USA) compote on slender stem, Green, £60/$60. 6" bowl on Clambroth base, £35/$35.

FRUITS AND FLOWERS (USN). Bon-Bon, Blue, £125/$125. Variant of three fruits.

GARLAND (USF) deep compote on three legs, external pattern, Green, £85/$85.

GOLDEN HARVEST (USI) decanter and stopper, Marigold on Clear, £90/$90.

GARDEN PATH (FRI) bowl showing internal pattern on Rio (Pink) Base Glass with Crackle exterior. £85/$155.

GLADER (aka STAR AND FAN) (SWE), bowl (small), Marigold £65/$115.

GODDESS OF THE HARVEST (USF)** bowl, Amethyst, not seen in UK, $6900 (no UK pricing). A prize piece. Ex-Fenton Art Glass Museum.

GOOD LUCK (USN) bowl, Cobalt Blue, Stipple Rays exterior, £400/$400.

GRAPE AND CABLE (USN). Fernery Shape, rare, Marigold, £850/$850. Also found with straight not curved sides.

GRAPE AND CABLE (USN) *butter and lid, Amethyst, £220/$220.*

GRAPEVINE LATTICE (USD) *bowl (small), Frosted on clear, £80/$80.*

(IMPERIAL) GRAPE (USI) punch bowl top and base, Green, £300/$300 Set.

VINTAGE GRAPE (USD) *rose bowl, Amethyst, £65/$65.*

GREEK KEY AND SCALES *(USN). Exterior pattern to compote on short stem, Green, £80/$80.*

GRAPE ARBOR (USD) *Master bowl, Amethyst, £250/$250. Northwood also made a pitcher with this pattern name.*

(HEAVY) GRAPE (USI). *plate, Helios Green, £85/$85.*

(MASSIVE) GRAPE, *Japanese reproduction 1980s, extra large bowl, Green base £85/$155.*

GREEK KEY (USN) *bowl, Green, with Bronze iridescence over, £90/$90.*

GRAPE ARBOR (USD) *Master bowl, Amethyst, Exterior pattern shown here.*

(HELIOS) GRAPE (USI) *bowl, Green, 'Helios Iridescence', £65/$65.*

(VINTAGE) GRAPE (USF) *bowl on Red base, 8", £2000+/$2000.*

GRAVEYARD SPHERE (SWE). *Commemorates a death in 1918. Made before era of Eda Lustre Ware Production. Item not on sale market.*

GREEK KEY AND SUNBURST (HRL?) vase on pedestal base, two handles, Marigold, £65/$120.

GRETA (HRL) milk jug, Marigold on Clear, £28/$50. In Royal Leerdam Pressed Glass Catalogue 1930s.

HANS (HRL) compote on short stem, mirror like Selenium finish, here on Yellow base, £85/$155 (also seen on Clear base, $35/$65).

HAND VASE (EUR). Pair of vases, version with watch on wrist, Marigold on Clear, £85/$155 each.

HAMBURG (SWE). Named ex-Eda Catalogue, Banana Boat Shape, Blue, £425/$765. Variation on Randel.

HAND VASE (CZA). Extremely rare iridised acid etched Green based ('Camphor') glass with clear iridescence over. No watch on wrist of hand. £385/$695.

HATTIE (USI) aka **BUSY LIZZIE** bowl, Marigold on Clear, £35/$35.

HEADDRESS (SWE). Interior pattern to Curved Star, compote, Blue frilled edge $85, ground edge base collar. Also found inverted as base to Punch bowl set.

HAZEL vase, manufacturer not known, found at Eda Sweden but not proved source, Marigold on Clear, £65/$115.

HEARTS AND FLOWERS (USN) bowl, Ice Blue, (rare), £800/$800.

HEARTS AND FLOWERS (USN) plate, 9", Green, very rare this colour, £2500/$2500.

HEARTS AND FLOWERS *(USN)**. Tall-footed compote, circa 1920, Ice Blue, £2000/$2000. Profile view. Ex-Fenton Art Glass Museum.*

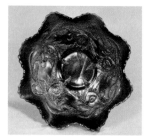

HEARTS AND HORSESHOES *(USF) bowl, Green, very rare, £850/$850.*

HEARTS AND TREES *(USF)**. Here as interior pattern to* **BUTTERFLY AND BERRY** *Master bowl on three knob feet, £135/£135 with interior pattern as noted. Ex-Fenton Art Glass Museum.*

HEART AND VINE *(USF)** plate, 9", Blue, £480/$480. Ex-Fenton Art Glass Museum.*

(JEWELLED) HEART *Whimsey (USD) plate with sides pulled up into eight points. Amethyst, pattern on exterior, £565/$565. A one-off.*

(STREAM OF) HEARTS *(USF)** compote with double crimped edge, Marigold, with* **PERSIAN MEDALLIONS** *exterior, £220/$220. Ex-Fenton Art Glass Museum.*

HEAVY CUT *(FRI) Banana Boat shape large bowl, Marigold on Clear £85/$155. Shown on Cat with base to make a Punch bowl.*

HERRINGBONE AND IRIS, *Jeanette (USA) Depression Ware water set, Marigold on Clear. Pitcher £125/$125, pedestal base tumblers £65/$65 each.*

HOBNAIL BANDED *(EML) tumblers, both rare. Marigold £680/$1225, Blue £800/$1440.*

(SWIRLED) HOBNAIL *(USM)** rose bowl, Amethyst, circa 1910, £285/$285. Ex-Fenton Art Glass Museum.*

HOBNAIL *(USM) rose bowl, Amethyst, £350/$350.*

HOBSTAR AND FEATHER *(USM)** giant rose bowl, 8½" high, circa 1910, Amethyst, £2000/$2000. Ex-Fenton Art Glass Museum.*

HOBSTAR AND CUT TRIANGLES (ESB) large shallow bowl, Amethyst, £75/$135.

HOBSTAR AND TASSELS (USI) bowl (small), Amethyst, £155/$155, hard to find.

HOBSTAR FLOWER (USN) compote, Green, £250/$250.

(CARNIVAL) HOLLY (USF) bowl on Red base £2000/$2000.

HOLLY AND BERRY (USD) bowl Amethyst, £70/$70.

HOLLY SPRIG (USF). Hat shape, Green, £125/$125.

HONEYCOMBE AND CLOVER (USF) external pattern to Feathered Serpent bowl, 10" Blue, £125/$125.

HORSES HEADS (USF) footed bowl, close-up, Blue, £210/$210.

*IDYLL vase (USF).** WATERLILY AND CATTAILS with BUTTER-FLY. Loaned to Fenton Art Glass Museum By Mr and Mrs S Myers. Value £450+/$450.*

INGA VASE (SWE) fine blow-moulded iridised and etched, Marigold on Clear, £85/$155..

ILLUSION (USF). Bon-Bon, two-handles, Blue, £78/$78.

IRIS (USF) compote on long stem, Green, £48/$48.

JET BLACK BEAUTY (FRI) plate, two open edge handles, eight-sided on rare Jet base. Extremely rare Art Deco style end of Carnival Glass period, akin to Fostoria USA Designs, £1650/$2970.

KAREN (SWE) deep bowl, Pale Blue base, £185/$335.

KITTENS (USF) cup and saucer, Marigold, £180/$180 for pair. Spooner, Marigold, £125/$125.

KOHINOOR (ENG) shallow Marigold bowl, 6", $30, aka **BEVELLED DIAMONDS AND BEADS**. £30/$55.

KOKOMO (ENG) rose bowl on stubby legs, Marigold on Clear, £35/$65. Also found (rarely) in Amethyst.

JETTA (FRI) vase on Jet base glass, Art Deco style as Jet Black Beauty plate. Blow moulded vase, Very Rare £650/$1170.

KANGAROO (AUS) small deep bowl, Marigold, hand-worked edge, £165/$300.

KINGFISHER (AUS). Crown Crystal Glass Sydney, bowl, 9"+, Marigold, £175/$315, with mould No Rd418. 4. Courtesy Museum Applied Arts and Sciences Sydney.

KOOKABURRA (AUS)*** bowl 9" with stippled centre, Black Amethyst, £325/$585.

JULIANA (EMK) Blue-base vase, Rare, £450/$810. Courtesy Estonian Sources. See Acknowledgements.

KINGFISHER (AUS)*** bowl, hand-worked edge, variant of Kookaburra design, Black Amethyst, £325/$585.

KIWI (AUS)***. Two small compotes with **SCROLL & DAISY** exterior. Black Amethyst £325/$585, Marigold £225/$405.

KULOR VASE (SWE). A very rare Milk Glass with clear iridescence over. £1000/$1800. Also on Marigold and Blue Base (£165/$300).

LAGERKRANTZ (SWE). Bonbonniere with lid, Blue, £850/$1550.

*LATTICE AND GRAPE (USF)** water set, 1912, Blue, pitcher £325/$585, tumbler £95/$95. Ex-Fenton Art Glass Museum.*

LEAF AND BEADS (USN) rose bowl, Ice Green, £400+/$400.

LEAF CHAIN (USF) bowl, soft Marigold iridescence, £48/$48.

LEAF CHAIN (USF) bowl, Blue, £75/$75.

*LILY OF THE VALLEY (USF)** water set, Blue, Pitcher alone £4000/$4000. Ex-Fenton Art Glass Museum.*

LONDON (SWE). Named from Eda Catalogue, Deep bowl, Marigold, £165/$300.

LONG HOBSTAR (USI) punch bowl and base, Marigold, £150/$150.

LION (USF) small bowl, Blue, 7", £300/$300.

LOTUS AND GRAPE (USF) Bon-Bon, two-handled Marigold, £100/$100.

LOUISA, Jeanette (USA) Depression Ware water set, Marigold, Pitcher £125/$125, tumbler £38/$38.

MAGDA (FRI) Candlesticks, blow moulded, Ice Blue, pair £480/$850.

MAPLE LEAF (USD). Small stemmed 4" compote Fruit, Amethyst, £48/$48.

MARTHA (ENG?) deep bowl, Marigold on Clear, £38/$70.

MAUD (SWE) shallow bowl, flared sides, Blue, £265/$480.

MIKADO (USF) giant compote on stem, aka **MASSIVE CHERRY** compote, Marigold on Clear £250/$250.

Right: **MITRED DIAMONDS AND PLEATS** (ESB) bowl, Marigold £25/$45 (and see small pin tray under **DIAMONDS AND PLEATS**).

MARBLES. Modern iridised marbles on Old Bone Marble Board, £285/$515 complete.

MARY ANN (USD) two-handled vases, Marigold £100/$100, Amethyst £250/$250. Very rare three-handled version was made.

MAYAN (USM) shallow bowl, Green, £165/$165. Marigold bowl extremely rare.

MEYDAM (HRL) cake plate on short stem, Marigold on Clear, mirror-like (Selenium) Finish, £68/$120. Ex-Royal Leerdam Catalogue, named after chief designer Floris Meydam.

MARILYN (USM)** pitcher, Amethyst, circa 1910, £1000/$1000. Highly sought after in USA. Ex-Fenton Art Glass Museum.

MATCHBOX HOLDER (FRI) in Riihimaki Catalogue 1930s, Marigold on Clear £65/$115, rare.

MEMPHIS (USI) punch bowl top and base, Marigold, £300/$300.

MILADY (USF)** water set, Catalogue No 1110, in Marigold, pitcher £350/$630, tumbler £90/$90. Ex-Fenton Glass Museum USA.

MÖLLER *(SWE) large bowl, Blue, flared out shape, £325/$585.*

MY LADY *(EUR) powder bowl, and lid, Marigold on Clear, £80/$145.*

NAUTILUS *(USD) shell shaped bowl on Peach Opalescent, £350/$350. From an old Northwood mould.*

NUTMEG GRATER *(SWE/Poss HRL/ESB). All Marigold on Clear, stemmed sugar £38/$70, butter and lid £68/$120, pedestal base creamer £28/$50.*

NUTMEG GRATER *(SWE) flared-edge bowl, Marigold on Clear, £85/$155.*

MOONPRINT *(UK/Scandinavia) creamer, Marigold on Clear, £28/$50.*

NANNA *(SWE) vase, Marigold on Clear, £165/£300.*

NIPPON *(USN) shallow bowl, clear frosted, £300/$300.*

OCTET *(USN) bowl, 8" Amethyst, £110/$110.*

MORNING GLORY *(USM)** water set, Marigold, Pitcher £8000/$8000, tumbler £900/$900. One of the rarest sets in Carnival Glass. Ex-Fenton Glass Museum.*

NANTIA *(SWE) plate, Marigold, £265/$480.*

NORA VASE *(EMK). Poorly iridised version but rare, £68/$120. Courtesy Estonian sources, see acknowledgements.*

OLGA *(SWE) bowl, Collar base ground, Marigold, £65/$115.*

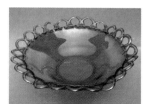

OLIVIA, possibly Val St Lambert Belgium copy of USI model. Giant bowl 12"+, thin glass, open Tulip edge, Marigold on Clear, £165/$300. Often seen in Belgium.

ORANGE TREE ORCHARD (USF)** pitcher, Blue, £450/$450. Ex-Fenton Art Glass Museum.

ORNATE BEADS (FDK). Two Candlesticks, four-section mould, Blue, Catalogue No 4863. Limited output, £860/$1550 Pr. Photo Courtesy Karhula Museum.

PANELLED DANDELION (USF)** water set, Amethyst, Butler Bros Cat 1910. Pitcher £600/$600, tumbler £85/$85. Ex-Fenton Art Glass Museum.

OPEN EDGE BASKET (USF) punch bowl and base, Amethyst.

ORANGE TREE (USF)** water set variant, Catalogue No 1402, 1911. Deep Blue, pitcher £400/400+, tumbler £150/$150. There is also an earlier pitcher. Ex-Fenton Art Glass Museum.

OWL Money Box (poss SWE/CZA). Marigold on Clear, £45/$80.

PANELS AND THUMBPRINTS (USI) compote on short stem, Amethyst, £48/$48.

ORANGE TREE (USF) hatpin holder, Blue based, £380/$380.

ORIENTAL (China). Modern blown iridised ginger jar with lid, etched pattern here with original box £38/$70.

PALM BEACH (USD) rose bowl, Amethyst, £48/$48.

PANSY (USI) Nappy, Clear White Frosted. This is an Imperial Reproduction Colour, £45/$45.

(AUSTRALIAN) PANSY (AUS)*** *small straight edged crystal bowl with design set Intaglio in base and iridised. Similar to Cherub and Cicled Rose, £165/$300.*

PEACOCK AT THE FOUNTAIN (USN) tumbler, blue, £110/$110.

PEACH AND PEAR (USD) *Banana Boat Shape, Amethyst, £145/$145.*

PANTHER (USF). *Master bowl on three legs, blue, £275/$275. Rare in Green (£800/$800)*

PANELLED SUGAR (AUS)***. *Crown Crystal Glass Sydney, sugar, Black Amethyst base, £65/$115. Here with a sugar, panelled sugar, on Marigold £060/$100.*

PEACOCK AND DAHLIA (USF) *bowl, Ice Blue, £200/$200, scarce.*

PEACOCK AND DAHLIA (USF) *bowl, reverse side shown, Ice Blue, £200/$200, scarce.*

PEACOCK AND URN (USF)** *compote, crimped edge, 1915, Marigold on Aqua, £250/$250. Ex-Fenton Art Glass Museum.*

PEACOCK AND GRAPE (USF) *bowl with spatula feet, on Amberina base, £1250/$1250.*

PEACOCK AND GRAPE (USF) *bowl on Vaseline base with Marigold iridescene over, £680/$680.*

PEACOCK AND URN (USF) *bowl, interior face clear iridised on Milk Glass. Exterior:* **BEARDED BERRY** *pattern with Marigold iridescence over. A one-off experimental piece. £3000+/$3000.*

PEACOCK AND URN *(USN) so marked bowl, Ice Cream, Cobalt Blue, £150/$150.*

PEACOCK AND URN *(USF)**. Profile of compote No 229 Marigold on Aqua Base, £250/$250. Ex-Fenton Art Glass Museum.*

PEACOCK ON THE FENCE *(USN)** plate, Ice Blue, extra rare, £1000+/$1000. Ex-Fenton Art Glass Museum.*

PEACOCK TAILS *(USF) Bon-Bon, Amethyst, £75/$75.*

PEACOCK ON THE FENCE *(USN) bowl, Frosted White, clear iridised. Price Not known.*

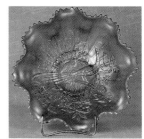

PEACOCK ON THE FENCE *(USN)** bowl, 8″, Marigold on Aqua, £200/$200. Ex-Fenton Art Glass Museum.*

PEACOCK ON THE FENCE *(USN) plate, Blue, £1000+/$1000.*

(STRUTTING) PEACOCK, *West-moreland USA. creamer, Amethyst, £85/$155.*

PEBBLE AND FAN *(CZA) giant vase, blow moulded on Vaseline with Marigold iridescence. Value £1200/$2160. Also found Marigold on Clear at $800/$1400.*

PERSIAN MEDALLIONS *(USF) bowl, hand-worked edge, Green 8″+, £75/$75 with hand-worked edge.*

PERSIAN MEDALLIONS *(USF)** punch bowl (top only), Blue, with base £360/$360. Ex-Fenton Art Glass Museum.*

PERSIAN MEDALLIONS *(USF). Two compotes: Marigold on clear stem £85/$85; Blue £60/$60.*

PETER RABBIT (USF)** plate 102, Blue, circa 1912, Bearded Berry exterior, £3600/$3600. Ex-Fenton Art Glass Museum.

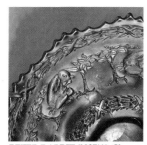

PETER RABBIT (USF)**. Close up of plate. Ex-Fenton Art Glass Museum.

PINCHED SWIRL (USD) small vase, pinched top, Peach oplaescent, £100/$100.

PIN-UPS (AUS)*** wide flared bowl, Marigold on clear, Interior pattern, £185/$335.

PINEAPPLE ROYAL (EUR) vase, Marigold on Clear, £35/$65.

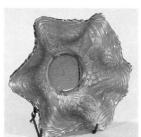

PINE CONE (USF) (aka **FIR CONE**) bowl, Marigold, £45/$45.

PINWHEEL (ESB) vase (large), Amethyst 8", £125/$225. Small Marigold vase (6½"), £38/$70, from Sowerby Derby Suite.

PLAID (USF) bowl 8", Ice (Celeste) Blue, very rare £1200/$1200.

POINSETTIA (USN)** bowl, three-toed 9", Blue, £800/$800. Ex-Fenton Art Glass Museum.

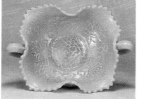

POINSETTIA (USN) bowl, Amethyst are in USA £465/$465.

Right: **POND LILY** (USF)** Bon-Bon, pattern view, rare Opaque Blue. Catalogue No 1414 circa 1923, loaned to Fenton Art Glass Museum By Mr and Mrs M E Cain.

POND LILY (USF) Bon-Bon, clear frosted, £125/$125.

Po–Qu

PONY *(USD) bowl, Marigold over Aqua, a one-off. $1250/$1250.*

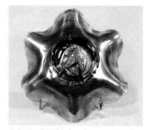

PONY *(USD) bowl, exterior view showing Aqua to picture on left.*

POPPY SHOW *(USN) plate, Yellow base glass,* **BASKETWEAVE** *exterior, £3000/$3000.*

POWDER BOWL *(Bambi) (EUR) with lid, Marigold on Clear, £65/$115.*

PRISMA *(SWE) ex-Eda Lyster catalogue, 1925, bowl, shallow, Blue, £185/$335.*

QUARTER BLOCK *(EUR probably ESB). Depression Era Ware: creamer, sugar, butter and lid. All on Marigold. Set £95/$180.*

QUANDRY *(SWE) bowl, deep Shape, Blue, £165/$300. Similarities with Queenie and Quiver.*

QUATTRO (SWE). Named ex-Eda Catalogue, bowl, Marigold, £165/$300.

QUANTUM (SWE) vase, Blue, £365/$660.

QUEENIE (SWE) Similarities with Quandry & Quiver bowl, deep within, turned top, Blue, £265/$480.

QUESTION MARKS *(USI) compote on short stem, Amethyst, £48/$48.*

QUILTED FANS, Fii. Oblong dish, Blue base, Iittala Catalogue No 4800. Only known piece in this shape and colour to date, £850/$1550. Courtesy Suomen Lasimuseo, Finland.

QUINCE (SWE) water jug, pale iridisation, blow moulded, £85/$155.

QUIVER (SWE) bowl, Blue £225/$405. Variation on Quandry and Queenie.

(STIPPLED) RAYS (USN) bowl, Amethyst, N mark in circle within centre of bowl. Deep Purple. Northwood made no Red. £48/$48. +15% for Northwood Mark.

REX (SWE) vase, Milk glass base, pinched in top, £1000/$1800. A rarity in this base glass.

RIBBONS AND LEAVES (ENG) straight sided small dish with two handles, unusual base pattern, Marigold on Clear, £38/$70.

RIBBON SWAGS (USN) bowl on three legs, Amethyst, £125/$125. WISHBONE interior.

RIBBON SWIRL, often found in Belgium. Possibly copy of COLUMBIA (USI) Pattern. 13" Cake plate on flared column stem, Marigold on Clear £150/$150.

RIBBON TIE (USF)** fruit bowl, 9", crimped edge, circa 1911, Blue, £280/$280, Add 25% for a crimped edge. Ex-Fenton Art Glass Museum.

RIBBON TIE (USF) bowl, Amethyst, collar base $190/$190. Crimped edge add 25%.

RIIHIMAKI (FRI) tumbler with name Riihimaki raised in base. Blue, £2880/$5185.

RIIHIMAKI (FRI) tumbler showing raised base name.

ROSALIND (USM)** compote, with diving dolphin feet, Amethyst £650/$650. Ex-Fenton Art Glass Museum.

ROCCOCO WAVES (EUR) oil lamp on metal base. Glass Pale Lilac, Smoke with soft iridescence over.

Ro

(BASKET OF) ROSES *(USD?)* *Bon-Bon with rare stippled background, Amethyst, £120/$120.*

(CAPTIVE) ROSE *(USF) plate on Blue, 10", £295/$295.*

(CAPTIVE) ROSE *(USF) Bon-Bon, Blue, £85/$85.*

(CIRCLED) ROSE *(AUS)*** Clear crystal dish with Intaglio iridised pattern in base. With Australian Pansy and Golden Cupid. £165/$300 each.*

(FINE CUT AND) ROSES *(USN) exterior pattern to small bowl, Amethyst, £125/$125.*

(OPEN) ROSE *(USI) bowl, footed, Amethyst, £45/$45.*

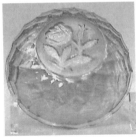

(QUILTED) ROSE *(EUR). Base of bowl. £65/$115*

ROSE PANELS *(EUR). Large bowl on fixed column base, Marigold on Clear, £125/$225. Possibly Dutch, favouring Rose patterns.*

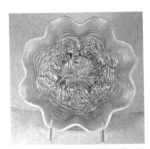

ROSE SHOW *(USN)** bowl with* **REEDED BASKETWEAVE** *exterior, on Aqua Opal Base, £1500+/$1500.*

ROSE WREATH *(USD) rose bowl, Marigold, £40/$40.*

ROSOR *(SWE) large size letter vase ex-Eda 1929 catalogue. Blue base £1600/$2880 and smaller size $1200/$2160. Also found on non-iridised Red base.*

ROSOR *(SWE) large pitcher, Blue, £950/$1710.*

TEXTS ROSE (USD) amethyst, showing domed base. £65/$65.

ROWBOAT *(ESB) celery dish, Marigold iridated on Aqua. Very rare, £300/$540.*

SAILBOATS *(USF) goblet, Marigold, £200/$200. wine glass, Marigold, £45/$45.*

SEACOAST *Spittoon (USM). Here as souvenir repro piece for American Carnival Glass Association. Peach Opalescent, Base reads 'Dayton Ohio 1982' with central insignia of ACGA, £75/$75.*

(WILD) ROSE (USN) bowl on three knob feet and open-edge Tulip Top. Amethyst, £75/$75.

ROUND-UP *(USDD) plate, 9", hand-worked edge, with BIG BASKETWEAVE exterior, Amethyst £220/$220 with worked edge.*

SCALE BAND *(USF)** pitcher No 212 Fenton Model, circa 1908, £350/$350. Ex-Fenton Art Glass Museum.*

SEAWEED *(USM)** bowl, 10", crimped, Green, circa 1910, £880/$880. Ex-Fenton Art Glass Museum.*

(WREATH OF) ROSES (USF)** punch set with PERSIAN MEDALLIONS interior, Blue, £400/$400 Set. Ex-Fenton Art Glass Museum.

SAILBOATS *(USF) small bowl, 6", Green, £75/$75.*

SCROLL EMBOSS *(USI) bowl, Amethyst 8", £65/$65. This pattern adopted by Sowerby UK in some cases.*

SEAWEED AND CORAL (CZA?) four-sided vase, marigold iridescence on clear, decorated Carnival on Crackle base glass. £1850/$3330.

SHELL *(USI) bowl, 9", Amethyst, £100/$100.*

(FEATHERED) SERPENT *(USF) bowl, 10", Amethyst, £48/$48.*

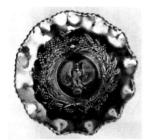

SHRIKE *(AUS)*** bowl, 6", hand-worked edge, Black Amethyst, £260/$470.*

SIX PETALS *(USD)** bowl, crimped edge, Purple, circa 1912, £85/$85. Ex-Fenton Art Glass Museum.*

SMALL RIB *(USD) rose bowl, on clear stem, Marigold frilled top, £65/$65.*

SMOCKING *(USA). Modern Carnival Glass, Indiana Glass Co. Powder bowl and Lid on Deep Blue, £48/$48. Named by Lorna Payne (UK).*

SMOOTH RAYS PANELS *(USI) plate, Smoke, eight-sided, £125/$125.*

SONYA (SWE) bowl on Rio (Pink) base, £0000/$000.

SOPHIA *(SWE) pedestal based vase, Soft Amber base, £195/$350.*

SOLDIERS AND SAILORS *(USF)** commemorative plate 7½", Blue base, £2200+/$2200. Courtesy late Don Moore USA.*

SNOW FANCY, *McKee (USA) creamer and pitcher, Marigold, £65/£65 each.*

SPIRIT OF '76 (USA). Commemorative plate on Yellow base, £38/$38.

SPRINGTIME (USN)**, all Amethyst, creamer £400/$400, sugar £400/$400, butter £400/$400, Pitcher £880/$880. Ex-Fenton Art Glass Museum.

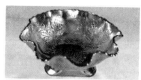

STAG AND HOLLY (USF) bowl on spat feet, Red Base, £2000/$2000.

SPRINGTIME (USN)** water set, extremely rare pattern, Green pitcher £950/$950, tumbler £200/$200. Ex-Fenton Art Glass Museum.

(CURVED) STAR (SWE). Inverted stemmed sugar (ground base) with bowl top, Blue, £265/$475. Set of two pieces.

STAG AND HOLLY (USF)** Master bowl, 13", Green, £680/$680. Ex-Fenton Art Glass Museum.

(CURVED) STAR (SWE), here as Dagny vase, Blue, £310/$560.

(DOUBLE) STAR (FDK) sugar bowl, Blue, interior plain, £125/$225. Courtesy Karhula Lasimuseo

(EASTERN) STAR (USI?) compote on stem, Marigold, with SODA GOLD exterior pattern. Riihimaki Finland also used this pattern on Rio base, £38/$38 on clear base glass.

(MANY) STARS (USM), 10" crimped bowl, circa 1910, Marigold, £400/$400 + 25% for crimped edge.

(SPINNING) STAR (FDK). Three vases, Blue turned in or flared lip. Catalogue Nos 4888/4889. Value £310/$560 each. Courtesy Karhula Lasimuseo.

STAR AND FAN (SWE) vase, Blue £325/$585.

STAR AND FILE (USI) decanter and stopper, Marigold, £110/$110.

STAR AND HOBS (SWE) extra large Banana Boat bowl, Blue, £365/$660.

STAR AND STUDS (ESB) bowl, shallow, splayed on three legs, Marigold, £48/$85.

STAR AND OVALS (FRI) in Finnish Riihimaki Catalogue, 1930s, Marigold creamer £28/$50.

STARS AND PENDANTS (EML?) small compote on stem, Marigold on Clear. Found Estonia, £85/$155 (rare). Courtesy Estonian sources, see acknowledgements.

STARBURST (FRI) sugar and milk, Blue, Riihimaki Nos 5682/5683. £85/$155 Each.

STARDUST (EML) bowl, Marigold, Small, £85/$155. Courtesy Estonian sources, see acknowledgements.

STARBURST MEDALLIONS (EML) bowl, Blue, £225/$405. Courtesy Estonian sources, see acknowledgements.

STARBURST AND CROWN (EML) long-stem compote, Blue, extra rare £365/$660. Same design in Finland. Courtesy Estonian sources, see acknowledgements.

STARFLOWER (USF)** pitcher, three pint, Blue, circa 1911, £1500/$1500. Ex-Fenton Art Glass Museum.

STARLIGHT (EML) vase, Marigold, £135/$245. Courtesy Estonian sources, see acknowledgements.

STAR OF DAVID (USI) bowl, scarce in Amethyst, ARCS exterior. £250/$250.

STAR OF DAVID AND BOWS
(USN) bowl, Amethyst, £150/$150.

STARSTRUCK (SWE) bowl,
splayed-out top. See centre Base Star,
Blue, £365/$660.

STJARNA (SWE) Bonbonniere,
Blue, extremely rare, £1500/$2700.

(VERTICAL) STAR PANELS
(FDK), Bonbonniere with lid,
extremely rare, Blue, £1000/$1800.

STIPPLED RAYS (USF) extra large
(11") squared-off edges bowl frilled
top, Green, £465/$465.

STORK AND RUSHES (USD)
punch bowl top and base, Marigold,
£125/$125 set.

STRAWBERRY (USN)** bowl,
hand-worked edge, Marigold,
£105+/$105 add 25% for worked-
edge.

STRAWBERRY SCROLL (USF)
tumbler No 902, Blue, £280/$280.

(WILD) STRAWBERRY (USN)
small bowl, 6", one side upturned,
£150/$150.

SUMMERS DAY (USD) vase,
actually base to Stork and Rushes
punch set. Marigold, base vase only
here £80/$80.

SUNFLOWER (USN) bowl on spat
feet, Green 8", £65/$65.

SUNFLOWER AND DIAMONDS
(SWE) two vases, each on blue base
£380/$685.

SUNGOLD (EUR) shallow plate, thin glass, Marigold iridised. Described as Sungold by M Hartung. £125/$225.

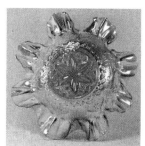

SUNGOLD FLORAL (EUR) bowl on thin glass, hand-worked frilled-edge, Marigold, £85/$155.

SUNSPRAY Epergne, origin not known. Bowl and central flute in metal holder, Marigold. Pattern as Sungold exterior M Hartung, Not Sungold Epergne as per Bill Edwards.

SVEA (SWE). Group: bowl $£8/$70, vase £58/$105, oblong pickle £48/$85, Small pin dish £28/$50, all Marigold.

(NESTING) SWAN (USM) large bowl, Marigold, with DIAMOND AND FAN exterior, £200/$200.

SWAN (AUS). Bowl on dark base. £235/$425.

SWATHE AND DIAMONDS (EUR) compote on stem, Marigold on Clear, £28/$50.

SWEDISH CROWN (SWE) bowl, straight sided, exterior pattern, Blue, £325/$585.

THISTLE (USF) bowl, Green base, £140/$140.

*TEN MUMS (USF)** water set, Blue, circa 1912, pitcher £800+/$800, tumbler £120/$120. Ex-Fenton Art Glass Museum.*

THISTLE (USF) Banana Boat shape bowl, Blue, scarce, £550/$550. Interior pattern WATERLILY AND CATTAILS.

THISTLE (EUR) vase, Marigold on Clear, £28/$50.

(GOLDEN) THISTLE pin tray (SWE?) on Crystal with iridised Intaglio base pattern, Golden, £260/$470.

THREE FOOTER (SWE) flared bowl on three legs, Blue, £000/$000.

THREE FRUITS (USN). Bon-Bon, twin-handles, Green £68/$68.

TIGER LILY (EML) pitcher in USA/Scandinavian pattern, Blue base, £420/$755. From Estonia, confirmed as local pattern from Melesk.

TOFFEE BLOCK pitcher, origin not known, chubby size, Marigold, £28/$50.

TOKIO (SWE) fluted bowl, blue, Reverse Swastika as symbol of Spring set intaglio in base £1850/$3330.

TROUT AND FLY (USM) bowl (shallow), Green £880/$880.

TREE TRUNK (USN) vase, (rare in Marigold) Amethyst £185/$185 .

TULIP AND CORD (FRI) mug with one handle, detailed background work, Marigold, Ex-Riihimaki Cat No 5150, £650/$1170. Courtesy Suomen Lasimuseo.

TRIO (SWE) bowl, large and shallow, exterior pattern, Blue £300/$540.

(REGAL) TULIP (EUR) Marigold vase on Pedestal base, £68/$120.

UNA (SWE) bowl, deep, external Geometric pattern, Marigold, $165/$300.

VINLOV (SWE) Banana Boat shape large bowl, very rare. Amethyst base, £1850/$3330.

VINTAGE (USF) bowl on Red base, £3000+/$3000. Very desirable piece.

WATER LILY (USF)** footed bowl, 6", No 1807, 1915, Amber base, £125/$125. Ex-Fenton Art Glass Museum.

TURKU (FRI). Commemorative ash tray on Rio base glass. Inscription reads: 'Jubilee of 1229, 1929 of the City of Turku. A souvenir made by O. Y. Riihimaki', £365/$660.

VERA (SWE) vase with round collared pedestal base, Blue, rare, £410/$740.

VINTAGE LEAF (USF) bowl Amethyst, £65/$65.

WATERLILY AND CATTAILS (USF) exterior to THISTLE Banana Boat. Blue £265/$265.

TWINS (USI) small bowl, 5", Marigold on Clear, £20/$20.

VINING LEAF, origin not known, perfume and stopper, Marigold on Clear, £85/$155.

WAFFLE BLOCK (USI) punch bowl base and top, Marigold, £185/$185 set.

WATERLILY AND DRAGONFLY (AUS)*** shallow wide bowl 10"+, Marigold on Clear, £160/$290.

WHIRLING LEAVES *(USM)** bowl, 9", Green with exterior fine Cut Ovals, £220/\$220. From Fenton Art Glass Museum.*

WHITE PITCHER *(USDD)** Crystal Pitcher, circa 1912, value not known. Fenton Art Glass Museum.*

WICKERWORK *(SWE). Group: three tripod bases, one Marigold iridised. Top and base set value Marigold iridised; £225/\$405. With Eda Mark value £525/\$875; Tripods Turquoise and Amethyst non-iridised. Top and base in White (Blanc de Lait) Milk Glass non-iridised.*

WICKERWORK *(ESB) upturned shallow bowl-cum-plate on tripod base, Marigold, £135/\$245, with Sowerby Peacock Trademark add \$50.*

WIDE PANELS *(USI) punch bowl set, Amethyst, as exterior to HEAVY GRAPE, £350/\$350.*

WILLS GOLD FLAKE *ash tray (ENG). The only known UK advertising piece of the period, £125/\$225.*

WINDFLOWER *(USD) bowl, 9", Blue, £58/\$58, add 25% for worked edge.*

WINDMILL *(USI) bowl, Amethyst, 9", £58/\$58.*

WINDMILL *(Variant): DOUBLE DUTCH (USI) bowl, 9", Clambroth, £110/\$110.*

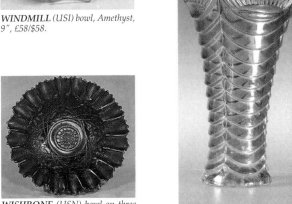

WISHBONE *(USN) bowl on three legs, with Ribbon Swags exterior, Green, £125/\$125.*

YORK *(SWE) vase, Marigold on Clear, £165/\$300.*

QUILT AND STAR (shorter of two vases) Blue base £395/$710, from Riihimaki Finland No 5934. STIPPLE AND STAR, (taller vase), No 5911. $365/$660. Courtesy Suomen Lasimuseo.

FOUR CROWNS plate, Pale Marigold, Karhula Finland, Catalogue No 4268 £165/$300. QUILTED PANELS tumbler, beaker in Marigold, three mould sections No 4020 (1926) £185/$335. Courtesy Suomen Lasimuseo.

STORK AND RUSHES tumbler (USD), £38/$38. GRAPE AND CABLE tumbler, £38/$38. **SODA GOLD** tumbler (USI), £28/$28; **TIGER LILY** (USI), £85/$85. **SINGING BIRDS** (USN), £45/$45; all in Marigold.

RIIHIMAKI tumbler (FRI) Blue, £2880/$5185. **CHERRY WREATH** whimsey, Amethyst 3" Black Amethyst, £750/$1350.

ENAMELLED CHERRIES (USF) tumbler, Blue, £135/$135. **FISHERMAN'S** (USDD) mug, Blue, £450/$450.

APPLE BLOSSOM (USD) bowl, Amethyst, £40/$40. **BLACKBERRY WREATH** (USM) small bowl £75/$75.

ZEPHYR decanter and handle, £65/$115. ZERO vase (SWE), £48/$85. ZINNIA decanter, no handle, £55/$100; all in Marigold. All blow moulded

STARBURST AND CROWN (FRI) tumbler, model 5047, Marigold, £265/$480. FLOWERSPRAY AND DIAMONDS (FRI) Tumbler model 5040 on Rio Glass, Marigold, £165/$300. Courtesy Suomen Lasimuseo Finland.

INTAGLIO STRAWBERRY, (USA). Souvenir mug, Modern. Vaseline Opalescent, £58/$58. **BEADED SHELL,** *American Carnival Glass Association Souvenir mug on Vaseline Base £58/$58. Motto: 'In God We Trust' inscribed on mug.*

SWAN AND CATTAILS Modern toothpick Holder. Blue, £48/$85. ELEPHANT mug, Modern, Blue, £58/$105.

BEADED PANELS *(USD) compote, Peach Opalescent, £85/$155.* **COMPASS** *(USD) exterior pattern compote on Peach Opalescent £85/$85.*

TOOLS *(SWE) from local collection, tools used in glass manufacture from Eda.*

INTAGLIO STRAWBERRY, repro American Carnival Glass Association piece, Blue, made by Fenton USA, £58/$105. **BUTTERFLY** *three-sided crimped dish, Modern, Blue, made by Fenton, USA, £48/$85.*

WILD ROSE *(USN) compote, open edge green on 3 knob feet, £85/$85.* **FINE RIB** *(USN) compote green, £48/$48.*

PANELLED DANDELION *(USF) tumbler, Amethyst, £85/$85.* **PEACH** *tumbler (USN), Blue (rare), £125/$125,* **BUTTERFLIES** *(USF) tumbler, Marigold, £38/$38.*

FLORENTINE *candlestick, acid etched, each* £62/$110. **PREMIUM** *(on Clear)* £85/$155 *each.*

Vases: **LEAF TIERS** *(USF), Amethyst,* £65/$65. **PULLED LOOP** *(USD), Peach Opalescent,* £125/$125, **FEATHERS** *(USN), Green,* £95/£95, **KNOTTED BEADS** *(USF), Green,* £68/$68.

ENAMELLED IRIS *tumbler (USF), aka* **ENAMELLED PRISM BAND** *Green,* £125/$125. **BEADED SPEARS** *tumbler (AUS), Marigold,* £120/$215.

(LARGE) **ROSE TUMBLER** *(EUR), Marigold,* £35/$65. **STRETCH** *tumbler (EUR),* £35/$65. **ORANGE TREE** *goblet (USF), Marigold,* $75/$75. **BLUEBERRY** *tumbler (USF), Marigold,* £85/$85. **DIAMOND PANES,** *Scandinavian, Marigold,* £5/£10.

BEADED BULLS EYE *(taller Vase) Amethyst,* £80/$145. **LONG THUMBPRINT** *vase (USD), Green,* £28/$28.

PANELLED DIAMONDS *tumbler (USF), Amethyst,* £88/$88. **VINTAGE BANDED TUMBLER** *(USD), Green (rare)* £600/$600. **ACORN BURRS** *tumbler (USN), Green,* £90/$90.

JACK IN THE PULPIT (CZA?) vase, Marigold, £40/$70. **HAND** *vase with watch on wrist (ELK), Marigold, £85/$155.* **DIAMOND POINTS** *vase (USN), Frosted White, £160/$160.*

DIAMOND WEDGES (SWE), small bowl, Blue, £165/$300. SALAD PANELS (SWE), larger bowl, Blue, £365/$660 Catalogue No 2229.

Punch cups: **WHIRLING STAR** *(EUR & USI), Marigold, £30/$55,* **BROKEN ARCHES** *(AUS), Marigold, £25/$45.* **WREATH OF ROSES** *(USF), £30/$30.*

FINE CUT RINGS, Guggenheim celery, produced under licence for UK market. Marigold, £65/$115. **FINE BAND** *celery vase, Marigold, £65/$115.*

WINDMILL *tumbler (USN), £28/$28.* **RANGER** *variant tumbler origin not known, £28/$28.* **GRAPE ARBOR** *tumbler (USN), £65/$65.* **INVERTED BLOCKS** *(EUR), £45/$80.* **FOUR, SEVEN, FOUR** *tumbler (USI), £40/$40.* **ROBIN** *(USI), scarce £60/$60. All Marigold.*

TOWN PUMP *Souvenir, Purple ICGA (USA) 1979, £58/$58. Dugan* **MANY FRUITS** *punch cup (USD), Amethyst, £35/$35.*

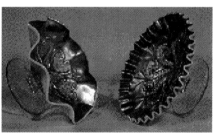

QUESTION MARKS *(USD) Peach Opalescent compote £68/$68.* **STARFISH** *(USD), Peach Oplaescent compote, £150/$150.*

BUTTERFLY *(CZA?) pin tray, Marigold, in two sizes, £18/$35 and £12/$20.* **BUTTERFLY** *perfume bottle, Modern Avon Glass, £12/$20.*

*All punch cups: **BROKEN ARCHES** (AUS), £25/$45; **WAFFLE BLOCK** (USI), £28/$28; **ORANGE TREE** (USF), £28/$28; **MEMPHIS** (USI), £35/$35, all Marigold.*

HEAVY GRAPE *goblet (USI), Marigold, £38/$38.* ***COLONIAL*** *(USI), one-handled punch cup, Marigold, £60/$60.*

GRAPE AND GOTHIC ARCHES *(USN), tumbler, Blue, £90/$90.* ***PEACOCK AT THE FOUNTAIN*** *(USD & USN), tumbler, Blue, £200/$200.*

BAVARIA CARAFFE (EUR), Marigold, £45/$80. INVERTED BLOCKS caraffe (EUR) Marigold, £45/$80.

GRAPE AND CABLE *(USF) tumbler, Amethyst, £48/$48. ZILLERTAL Beer Bottle, Modern, Amber based, £38/$70.* ***BANDED GRAPE AND FLOWERS*** *(USF), tumbler, Amethyst, £78/$78.*

Later production American Carnival Glass from L. E. Smith and Indiana Glass Co. catalogues.

Later production Carnival Glass from Indiana Glass Co.

Modern Fenton Art Glass under recent production – iridised crackle range.

Sketches and Drawings by Ron May

BEADED OVAL bowl with Tulip-shape edge, Marigold on Clear £35/$65.

BUTTON sandwich bowl, squared off sides exterior pattern, Marigold on Clear, akin to crosshatch, three mould marks, £28/$50.

CLAIRE (EUR) plate with underside clear iridised. Cut out. pointed shape edge to plate, £38/$70. Named by Ron May

CORNFLOWERS, deep bowl on short legs, often seen mon-iridised in acid Etched Green or Pink Depression Ware Glass. This bowl has external pattern and good iridisation, £58/$105. Marigold on Clear.

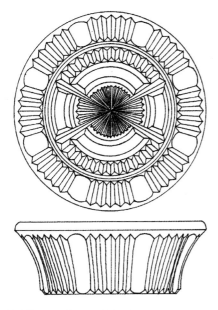

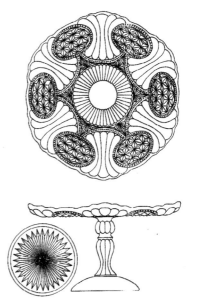

CROSS SECTION, small bowl, Marigold on Clear, £22/$40.

DIAMOND OVALS AND BEADS, cake stand on shaped column leg. Three mould marks, exterior pattern only, probably Dutch £58/$105. Excellent mirror-like iridisation.

DIAMOND SPEARS bowl, 9" approx, Marigold, £28/$50.

DIAMOND FRILLS and DIAMONDS bowl 9", Marigold, £28/$50.

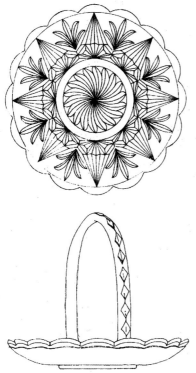

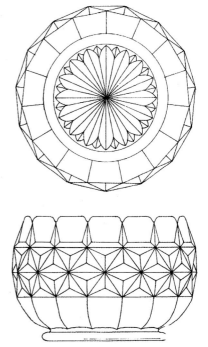

FACET BAND small deep Rose bowl turned in top, £20/$35. Marigold on Clear.

DUCHESSE Fleur de Lis pattern on upper side of English Basket shape. Slightly curved plate with arched handle running from one side to another. Very elaborate pattern and cut away design on handle, good iridescence, £48/$85.

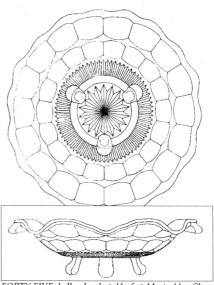

LAUREL WREATH, elegant compote, petal-like leaf design around outside, good iridescence, £48/$85, Marigold.

FORTY-FIVE shallow bowl, stubby feet, Marigold on Clear, £28/$50.

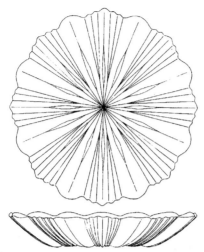

*PLEATS shallow bowl, Pale Marigold iridescence on Clear,
£18/£35.*

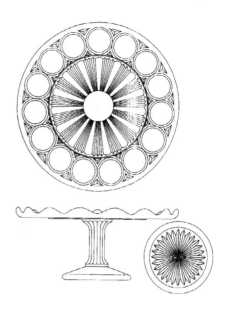

*ORBIT, Marigold iridised cake stand on a Ribbon column
stand Registration No 704493 (not Sowerby UK whose
registration numbers are prefixed RD and only up to
520894), £58/$105.*

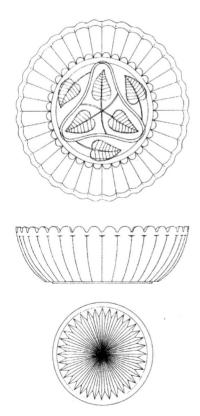

*LEAFY TRIANGLE, small bowl, with unusual leafy
triangle pattern in base (akin to Pillar Flute in some
respects) £48/$85. Marigold.*

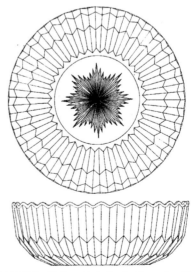

*ORIGAMI. Shallow fruit bowl, Depression Ware,
Marigold £18/$35.*

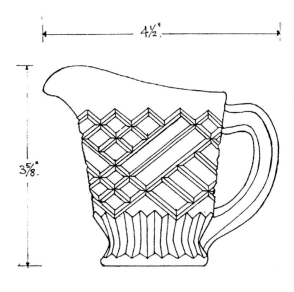

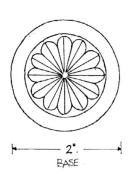

PARQUET small creamer, often poorly iridised, four mould marks, Intaglio cut out design, £28/$50, Marigold.

PETALS AND PRISMS small bowl, pattern of Crossed Petals and Small Dots and vertical prism bands, Pale Marigold on Clear, £28/$50.

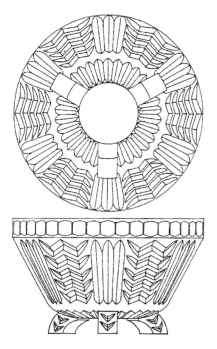

SPEARS AND CHEVRONS vase, Marigold on Clear £00/$00.

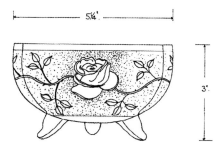

SERPENTINE ROSE *deep bowl on short legs, pattern external and stippled background, Soft Marigold over Clear* £65/$115.

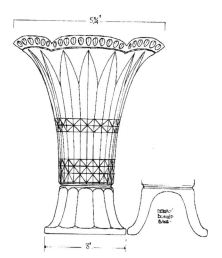

SPEARS AND DIAMONDS *Bands vase, flared or straight top found, akin to Triands in form, Marigold,* £28/$50.

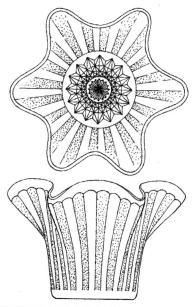

STIPPLED RAYS AND STARS, *small Marigold, rather hat-shaped star with 16 points in base* £28/$50.

ZIPPER-ROUND *aka* ZIP-A-ROUND *and* CHECKERBOARD. *Large shallow bowl, English, Marigold on Clear, very intricate design,* £58/$105.

Combined Index and Price Guide

NOTES FOR THE INDEX

1. Pieces shown in this book can all be found under the alphabetical pattern name sequence in this combined index and price guide.

2. The alphabetical sequence is arranged LETTER BY LETTER (not WORD BY WORD).

NOTES FOR THE PRICE GUIDE

Carnival Glass prices are always a thorny issue. Supply and demand remain the supreme market arbiters. However, for general guidance purposes, the prices in this book have been carefully compiled from pertinent Auction Houses, Antique Fairs and private sales in America and the UK. This GUIDE is simply that – and reflects prices reached at sale through the various outlets noted. Neither the Publisher, nor author, can be held responsible for any losses incurred in purchasing Carnival Glass using this Guide. Every effort has been made to give a fair and representative picture. Items not usually found in the UK (such as pastels) have been given estimated prices relating to the American dollar directly.

1. American pieces are priced in US$. For collectors in the UK, in order to translate into equivalent UK values, the £Sterling must be EQUATED with the quoted US$ price. This is to cover currency fluctuations, and post and package from America to the UK.

2. English and other NON AMERICAN pieces found in the UK ae quoted in £Sterling. To assist American readers, an approximate present day equivalent US$ value for such pieces follows after the £Sterling price. American readers must however realise that these comparison dollar prices for European pieces will vary with fluctuation in the currency markets.

3. Prices noted are mainly for pieces as shown in the book. A few examples may be given for other shapes, but space limitations have decreed that it has NOT been possible to produce a composite Price Guide for all shapes that can be found under the various patterns.

AFRICAN SHIELD
Manufactured by ESW***　　　　　　*Picture page 41*
Mustard Jar and Lid
Marigold £40/$70

ALEXANDER FLORAL (MQB)
Manufactured by FRI　　　　　　*Picture page 41*
aka GRAND THISTLE
Pitcher
Marigold £1260/$2270; Blue £1700/$3060
Tumbler
Marigold £200/$360; Blue £300/$540
Manufactured by EMK
Pitcher
Marigold £1250/$2250; Blue £1700/$3060
Tumbler
Marigold £200/$360; Blue £300/$540

AMERIKA
Manufactured by SWE. Named in Sweden (source)
Picture page 49
Bowl – stub feet
Marigold £150/$270; Blue £250/$450; Milk Irid £900/$1620
Rose bowl – stub feet
Marigold £150-200/$270-360; Blue £250-300/$360-$540;
Milk Irid £900/$1620

APPLE . . .

APPLE BLOSSOM
Manufactured by USD　　　　　　*Picture page 41, 78*
Bowl 4"
Marigold £25/$25; Amethyst £40/$40
Bowl 7"+
Marigold £25/$25; Amethyst £40/$40
Plate 8"+
Marigold £150/$150; Amethyst £170/$170;
Blue £180/$180

APPLE BLOSSOM TWIGS
Manufactured by USD**　　　　　　*Picture page 41*
Bowl 7½"
Amethyst £250/$250

APPLE PANELS
Manufactured in EUR　　　　　　*Picture page 41*
Creamer and/or Sugar
Marigold £30/$55

ARCS
Manufactured by USI　　　　　　*Picture page 41*
Exterior pattern to STAR OF DAVID
Bowl
Marigold £70/$70; Amethyst £250/$250; Green £180/$180

ARGYLE
Manufactured by HRL　　　　　　*Picture page 41*
aka TARTAN
Cake Plate on stem
Marigold £65/$115

ASHTRAYS
See *WILLS GOLD FLAKE*
See TURKU

ASTRID (MQB)
Manufactured by SWE　　　　　　*Picture page 41*
Bowl
Marigold £85/$155; Blue £185/$335

ATLANTIC CITY ELK
See ELK . . . ATLANTIC CITY ELK

ATHENA (MQB)
Manufactured by SWE　　　　　　*Picture page 42*
Bowl
Marigold £85/$155; Blue £185/$335

AUSTRALIAN CRYSTAL CUT (AUS)
Picture page 42
Compote
Black Amethyst £250/$45⸱

AUSTRALIAN PANELS (AUS)
Picture page 42
Creamer and Sugar s⸱
Marigold £80/$145; Black Amethyst £165/$300

AUSTRALIAN PANSY
See PANSY . . . (AUSTRALIAN) PANSY

AUSTRALIAN SWAN
See SWAN . . . (AUSTRALIAN) SWAN

AUTUMN ACORN
See ACORN... (AUTUMN) ACORN

BAMBI POWDER BOWL (EUR)
See POWDER BOWL BAMBI

BASKET OF ROSES (Tom Sprain, USA)
See ROSE . . . BASKET OF ROSES

BASKETWEAVE . . .

BASKETWEAVE
External pattern to WISHBONE　　　　*Picture page 42*

BIG BASKETWEAVE
Manufactured by USD
External pattern to ROUNDUP

BAVARIA (Frank Horn)
Manufactured in EUR　　　　　　*Picture page 82*
Marigold £45/$80

BEADED BASKET
Manufactured by USD　　　　　　*Picture page 42*
Marigold £35/$35; Amethyst £55/$55 Green £85/$85;
Blue £60/$60

BEADED BULLS EYE
Manufactured by USI　　　　　　*Picture page 80*
Vase
Marigold £30/$30; Amethyst £80/$80; Green £80/$80

BEADED CABLE
Manufactured by USN　　　　　　*Picture page 42*
Exterior pattern
Bowl – footed
Marigold £65/$65; Amethyst £85/$85; Green £125/$125

BEADED CRYSTAL & RAYS (Lorna Payne)
Manufactured in EUR?　　　　　　*Picture page 42*
Bowl – small
Marigold £20/$35

BEADED OVALS (Ron May)
Manufactured by HRL　　　*Drawing by Ron May page 84*
Bowl – shallow
Marigold £35/$65

BEADED PANELS
Dugan-Diamond, USA　　　　　　*Picture page 79*
Compote
Peach Opal £85/$85

BEADED SHELL
Manufactured by USD　　　　　　*Picture page 79*
American Carnival Glass Association Souvenir 1981
Vaseline Mug £60/$60

BEADED SPEARS
Manufactured in Australia   *Picture page 42, 80*
Pitcher
Marigold £360 / $650; Amethyst £460 / $830
Tumbler
Marigold £120 / $215; Amethyst £160 / $290

BEARDED BERRY
Manufactured by USF   *Picture page 42*
Exterior pattern to PETER RABBIT BOWL
Exterior pattern to PEACOCK AND URN

BEARS . . .

FROLICKING BEARS
Picture page 43
ICGA Award Reproduction Spitoon
Red £85 / $85

BEAUTY BUD TWIG VASE
Manufactured by USD   *Picture page 43*
Regular size
Marigold £65 / $65; Amethyst £85 / $85
Miniature size
Marigold £385 / $385; Amethyst £835 / $835

BELL & ARCHES
Manufactured by USD   *Picture page 43*
Bowl
Marigold £38 / $38; Blue £125 / $125

BERLIN
Manufactured by SWE   *Picture page 43*
Bowl
Marigold £155 / $280; Blue £235 / $425

BERRY & LEAF CIRCLE
Manufactured by USF
Exterior to LION bowl

BICENTENNIAL PLATE USA – SPIRIT OF 76
See SPIRIT OF 76

BIG BASKETWEAVE
Exterior pattern see BASKETWEAVE...

BIRDS . . .

BIRDS
Bowl – 9"
Marigold £210 / $380; Amethyst £300 / $540;
Blue £380 / $685 _

BIRDS & CHERRIES
Manufactured by USF   *Picture page 43*
Two-handled Bon-Bon
Marigold £45 / $45; Amethyst £80 / $80; Green £95 / $95;
Blue £95 / $95
Plate – 10"
Marigold £1000 / $1000; Green £1500 / $1500;
Blue £1500 / $1500
Bowl   *Drawing page 25*
£ / $ n / k _

BIRD WITH GRAPES
Manufacturer not known   *Picture page 43*
Wall Vase
Marigold £75 / $135 _

SINGING BIRDS
Manufactured by USN   *Picture page 43, 78*
Bowl – 10"
Marigold £60 / $60; Amethyst £70 / $70; Green £70 / $70
Bowl – 5"
Marigold £25 / $25; Amethyst £35 / $35; Green £45 / $45;
Blue £70 / $70

Mug
Marigold £125 / $125; Amethyst £190 / $190;
Green £380 / $380; Blue £190 / $190
Butter/Sugar/Creamer
Marigold £60 / $60
Spooner
Marigold £50 / $50
Pitcher
Marigold £200 / $200; Amethyst £225 / $225;
Green £350 / $350
Tumbler
Marigold £45 / $45; Amethyst £65 / $65; Green £125 / $125;
Aqua Opal (IG) £300 / $300

BLACKBERRY . . .

BLACKBERRY
Manufactured by USN   *Picture page 43*
Compote
Marigold £45 / $45; Amethyst £75 / $75; Green £85 / $85
Bowl – footed
Marigold £45 / $45; Amethyst £85 / $85 _ _ _ _ _ _ _ _ _ _ _

BLACKBERRY BLOCK
Manufactured by USF   *Picture page 43*
Pitcher**
Marigold £400+ / $400; Amethyst £1000+ / $1000;
Green £1000+ / $1000; Pastel £6000+ / $6000
Tumbler**
Marigold £48 / $48; Amethyst £150 / $150; Green £150 / $150;
Blue £150 / $270 _

BLACKBERRY WREATH
Manufactured by USM   *Picture page 78*
Amethyst £75 / $75 _

WILD BLACKBERRY
Manufactured by USF   *Picture page 43*
Bowl
Marigold £55 / $55; Amethyst £100 / $100;
Green £185 / $185

BLOCKS & ARCHES
Manufactured in Australia   *Picture page 81*
aka RANGER (Australia). See chapter on Australian production
Creamer
Marigold £28 / $50

BLUEBERRY **
Manufactured by USF   *Picture page 43, 80*
Pitcher
Marigold £400 / $400
Tumbler
Marigold £85 / $85; Blue £135 / $135

BORDERED PENDANT (MQB)
Manufactured by FDK   *Picture page 44*
Tumbler
Blue £350 / $630; Marigold £250 / $450

BOULE & LEAVES
See BULLS EYE & LEAVES

BOUQUET**
Manufactured by USF   *Picture page 44*
Pitcher
Marigold £300 / $300; Blue £650 / $650; White £800 / $800
Tumbler
Marigold £36 / $36; Amethyst £70 / $70; Blue £70 / $70;
White £100 / $100

BOWMAN
Named in Sweden (Source)   *Picture page 44*
aka NUTMEG GRATER (UK)
Deep Bowl
Marigold £85/$155; Blue £185/$335

BROKEN ARCHES
Manufactured by USI   *Picture page 44, 81, 82*
Punch Bowl & base
Marigold £180/$180
Punch Cup
Marigold £25/$25
Bowl 8"+
Marigold £25/$25

BROKEN CHAIN
See BUTTERFLY . . . BUTTERFLY & BOWER

BROOKLYN BRIDGE
Manufactured by USD   *Picture page 44*
Bowl – scarce
Marigold £140/$140
Unlettered bowl – rare
Marigold £800/$800

BULLS EYE & LEAVES
Manufactured by USN   *Picture page44*
aka BOULE AND LEAVES
Exterior pattern
Marigold £30/$30; Amethyst £35/$35; Green £35/$35

BUTTERFLY/BUTTERFLIES . . .

BUTTERFLIES
Manufactured by USF   *Picture page 44*
Tumbler
Marigold £38/$38; Amethyst £48/$48; Green £48/$48;
Blue £48/$48; White £70/$70
Bon Bon
Marigold £45/$45; Amethyst £55/$55; Green £55/$55;
Blue £55/$55

BUTTERFLY BOWL (MQB)
Modern   *Picture page 79*
3-sided bowl
Blue £48/$85

BUTTERFLY & BELLS
Manufactured in Australia   *Picture page 44*
Compote
Marigold £180/$335; Black Amethyst £240/$430

BUTTERFLY & BERRY
Manufactured by USF   *Picture page 44*
Bowl – footed 10"
Marigold £85/$85; Amethyst £185/$185; Green £185/$185;
Blue £200/$200
Bowl – footed 5"
Marigold £42/$42

BUTTERFLY & BOWER
Manufactured in Australia   *Picture page 44*
Exterior pattern to BROKEN CHAIN
Compote
Marigold £180/$335; Black Amethyst £240/$430
Cake Plate
Marigold £220/$400

BUTTERFLY & TULIP
Manufactured by USD   *Picture page 44*
Internal pattern to bowl
Boule – 10½" scarce
Marigold £300/$300; Amethyst £3000/$3000

Exterior pattern
Marigold £300/$300; Amethyst £3000/$3000

BUTTERFLY PERFUME
Modern USA (Avon)   *Picture page 81*
Marigold £12/$12

BUTTERFLY PIN TRAY
Picture page 81
Marigold £18/$35

BUTTON & HOB
Manufactured by ESW   *Picture page 44*
Bowl
Marigold £25/$45; Amethyst £65/$115; Blue £85/$155
Cake stand – 2 tier
Marigold £85/$155
Plate
Marigold £10/$20; Amethyst £35/$65

BUTTON SANDWICH (Ron May)
Manufactured by ESW   *Drawing by Ron May page 84*
Bowl – Squared-off
Marigold £28/$50

CANDLESTICKS . . .

FLORENTINE
Manufactured by ESW   *Picture page 45*
Acid etched
Marigold on clear £62/$110

OBSIDIAN
Manufacturer unknown   *Picture page 45*
Rare Jet Base Glass £260/$470 pair

ORNATE BEADS
Manufactured by FDK
Blue Base Glass £460/$830 pair

PREMIUM
Manufactured by USI   *Picture page 45*
Blue Base Glass £460/$460 pair

CANNON BALL
See CHERRY... ENAMELLED CHERRIES

CAPTIVE ROSE
See ROSE . . . CAPTIVE ROSE

CARAFFE . . .
See BAVARIA
See INVERTED BLOCKS

CARNIVAL HOLLY
See HOLLY . . . CARNIVAL HOLLY

CAR VASE (MQB)
Possibly manufactured by USI   *Picture page 45*
Marigold £35/$35

CATHEDRAL CHALICE
See STAR . . . CATHEDRAL CHALICE

CELIA (MQB)
Manufactured by FRI
Tumbler
Marigold £10/$20

CHARLIE (Source)
Manufactured by SWE   *Picture page 45*
Bowl
Marigold £165/$300; Blue £265/$480

CHECKERBOARD
Manufactured by ESW Drawing page 89
aka ZIPPER ROUND
Bowl
Marigold £38/$70

CHERRY/CHERRIES . . .

See also **BIRDS & CHERRIES**

- -

CHERRIES**
Manufactured by USM Picture page 45
Water Pitcher**
Marigold £800/$800; Amethyst £750/$750;
Green £1600/$1600
Tumbler
Marigold £80/$80; Amethyst £95/$95; Green £110/$110
Bowl – 4"
Marigold £50/$50; Amethyst £65/$65; Green £75/$75
Bowl – 7"
Marigold £50/$50; Amethyst £65/$65; Green £75/$75
Bowl – 10"
Marigold £60/$60; Amethyst £105/$105; Green £125/$125
Milk Pitcher (Rare)
Marigold £1200/$1200
Plate – 6"
Marigold £750/$750
Sugar/Creamer
Marigold £85/$85; Amethyst £135/$135; Green £135/$135

CHERRY
Manufactured by USD Picture page 45
Bowl – 5"
Marigold £40/$40; Amethyst £55/$55;
Peach Opal £125/$125; Red £650/$650
Bowl – 8"
Marigold £50/$50; Amethyst £65/$65;
Peach Opal £165/$165
Bowl – footed (scarce)
Marigold £180/$180; Amethyst £265/$265;
Peach Opal £300/$300; Red £650/$650
Plate – 6"
Amethyst £320/$320 Peach Opal £320/$320
Whimsey
Black Amethyst £650/$650

- -

CHERRIES & BLOSSOM**
Manufactured by USF Picture page 45,78
aka ENAMELLED CHERRIES
Pitcher
Marigold £280/$280; Blue £380/$380
Tumbler
Marigold £85/$85; Blue £135/$135

- -

CHERRY CHAIN
Manufactured by USF Picture page 45
Bon Bon
Marigold £40/$40; Amethyst £65/$65; Green £65/$65;
Blue £80/$145
Bowl 6", 10"
Marigold £65/$65; Amethyst £85/$85; Green £85/$85;
Blue £85/$85; Red £450/$450
Plate 7", 9" (rare)
Marigold £550/$550; Blue £225/$225

- -

ENAMELLED CHERRIES
See CHERRIES & BLOSSOM

- -

CHERRY WREATH
Manufactured by USD Picture page 78
Whimsey
Black Amethyst £750/$750

CHERUB
see ROSE... CIRCLED ROSE
Manufactured in Australia
See AUSTRALIAN PANSY (similar)

CHRISTMAS BELLS
See BUTTERFLY & BELLS

CHRYSANTHEMUM
Manufactured by USF Picture page 45
aka CHRYSANTHEMUM SPRIG
Master Bowl – 10" footed
Marigold £165/$165; Blue £285/$285

CHUNKY (MQB)
Manufactured by ESW Picture page 45, 46
aka ENGLISH HOB & BUTTON
Bowl
Marigold £30/$55; Blue £60/$110
Bowl – 2 tier
Marigold £90/$160; Blue £150/$270

CIRCLED ROSE
see ROSE . . . CIRCLED ROSE

CLAIRE (Ron May)
Manufactured in EUR Drawing by Ron May page 84
Plate – edge ¾" high
Marigold £38/$70

CLASSIC ARTS
Manufactured in Czechoslovakia Picture page 46
Vase 7"
Marigold £325/$585
Bowl
Marigold £325/$585
Powder Jar & Lid
Marigold £400/$720
Vase 10"
Marigold £400/$720

CLEMATIS
See ENAMELLED CLEMATIS

CLEVELAND MEMORIAL TRAY
Picture page 46
Marigold £4000/$7200; Amethyst £6000/$11000

COBBLESTONES
Manufactured by USI Picture page 46
See also ARCS exterior pattern
Bowl 5"
Marigold £28/$28; Amethyst £35/$35; Green £40/$40
Bowl 8"+
Marigold £48/$48; Amethyst £90/$90; Green £90/$90
Bon Bon
Marigold £48/$48; Amethyst £68/$68; Green £68/$68
Plate
Amethyst £1000/$1000

COIN DOT
Manufactured by USF Picture page 46
Bowl
Marigold £20/$20; Amethyst £55/$55; Green £55/$55;
Blue £65/$65; Pastel £100/$100; Red £1200/$1200;
on Aqua £260/$260
Plate
Marigold £160/$160; Amethyst £200/$200;
Green £220/$220; Blue £210/$210

Pitcher
Marigold £250/$450; Amethyst £400/$720;
Green £400/$720; Blue £400/$720
Tumbler
Marigold £100/$180; Amethyst £150/$270;
Green £150/$270; Blue £150/$270
Rose Bowl
Marigold £55/$100

COLONIAL
Manufactured by USI   *Picture page 82*
Punch Cup – single handle
Marigold £60/$60

COMMEMORATIVE PLATES
See SOLDIERS AND SAILORS
See SPIRIT OF '76

COMPASS
Manufactured by USD   *Picture page 79*
SKI STAR exterior to compote
Marigold £30/$30; Amethyst £60/$60; Green £60/$60;
Peach Opal £85/$85
Bowl – 10"
Marigold £60/$60; Amethyst £85/$85; Blue £160/$160;
Peach Opal £130/$130

CONCORD LATTICE
Manufactured by USF   *Picture page 46*
Bowl Green**
Marigold £85/$85; Amethyst £260/$260;
Green £360/$360; Blue £360/$360
Plate
Marigold £1500/$1500; Amethyst £3000/$3000;
Green £6000/$6000

COOKIE JAR & LID
see STAR . . . VERTICAL STAR PANELS

COOKIE PLATE
Manufactured by USI   *Picture page 46*
Pattern VINTAGE with a central handle
Smoke £185/$185

CORAL . . .

CORAL & SEAWEED
see SEAWEED & CORAL

CORN FLOWERS
Manufactured in EUR *Drawing by Ron May page 84*
Bowl – deep – 3 scroll feet
Marigold £58/$105

CORN VASE
HOACGA souvenir   *Picture page 46*
Ice Blue £78/$140

COVERED HEN
Manufactured by ESW   *Picture page 46*
Marigold £85/$155; Blue £300/$540

COVERED SWAN
Manufactured by ESW   *Picture page 46*
Marigold £135/$245; Blue £365/$660

CRACKLE
Manufactured by USI   *Picture page 47*
Car Vase
Marigold £65/$65; Amethyst £80/$80; Green £80/$80
Single Epergne
Marigold £85/$85
Bowl
Marigold £25/$25; Amethyst £30/$30; Green £30/$30

Pitcher
Marigold £90/$160; Amethyst £120/$215; Green £120/$215
Tumbler
Marigold £30/$55; Amethyst £35/$65; Green £35/$65
Punch Bowl Base
Marigold £85/$155
Punch Cup
Marigold £20/$35
Manufactured by FRI
Bowl
On pink base & *FOUR FLOWERS* internal
Rio £85/$155
as exterior to *GARDEN PATH* with *CRACKLE* and *SODA
GOLD*

CROSS HATCH
Manufactured in EUR   *Picture page 47*
Sugar on stem
Marigold £35/$65

CROSS SECTION (Ron May)
Manufactured in EUR *Drawing by Ron May page 85*
Bowl - small
Marigold £22/$40

CROW
Manufactured in Australia   *Picture page 47*
aka MAGPIE
Bowl
Marigold £180/$335; Black Amethyst £250/$450
Bowl
Marigold £180/$335; Black Amethyst £220/$400
Bowl variants
Marigold £180/$335

CRYSTAL CUT
See AUSTRALIAN CRYSTAL CUT

CUPID
See GOLDEN CUPID

CURVED STAR
Manufactured by SWE
aka DAGNY and LASSE
See STAR . . . CURVED STAR

CUSPIDOR
See SPITTOON

CUT ARCHES
Manufactured by FRI   *Picture page 47*
Banana Bowl
Marigold £85/$155; Blue £185/$335

CYNTHIA
Manufactured by ESW   *Picture page 47*
Vase – turned in rim short vase
Marigold £85/$155; Jet £850/$1550
Flared rim taller vase
Marigold £85/$155; Jet £850/$1550
Pair in Jet either size £2000/$3600;

DAGNY VASE
Manufactured by SWE   *Picture page 47*
See also STAR . . . CURVED STAR
Plain rim
Blue £365/$660
Flared rim
Blue £385/$695

DAINTY GOBLET (MQB)
aka GARLAND
Indiana USA modern production.
Blue £48/$85

DAISY...

DAISY & PLUME
Exterior pattern to BLACKBERRY _ _ _ _ _ _ *Picture page 47*

DAISY BLOCK ROWBOAT
See ROWBOAT
Marigold £65/$115; Amethyst £225/$405; Aqua £325/$585

DAISY SPRAY VASE (MQB)
Manufactured by SWE   *Picture page 47*
Bowl – shallow
Marigold £000/$000; Milk White Pearl £800/$1440
Vase – rim turned in
Marigold £185/$335; Blue £385/$695
Vase – flared rim
Marigold £165/$300; Blue £365/$660

DANDELION...

See also PANELLED DANDELION

Manufactured by USF   *Picture page 62*
Tumbler
Amethyst £85/$85

DECORATED CARNIVAL . . .
Manufactured by USF   *Picture page 48*
(1) No 1014** £nk/$nk
(2) No 1016 Water set** £nk/$nk

DERBY
See PINWHEEL

DIAMOND/DIAMONDS . . .

BANDED DIAMONDS
Manufactured in Australia
Water Pitcher (rare)
Marigold £750/$1350
Tumbler (rare)
Marigold £400/$720
Bowl 10"
Marigold £55/$100; Amethyst £65/$115
Bowl 5"
Marigold £35/$65; Amethyst £45/$80

DIAMANT (MQB)
Manufactured by SWE   *Picture page 48*
aka DIAMONDS
Bonbonniere
Blue £850/$1550
Vase – Plain lip
Marigold £165/$300; Blue £255/$460
Vase Flared Lip
Marigold £185/$335; Blue £285/$515

DIAMONDS
Manufactured by USM   *Picture page 48*
Pitcher **
Marigold £300/$300; Amethyst £380/$380;
Green £380/$380; Aqua £500/$500
Tumbler **
Marigold £70/$70; Amethyst £120/$120;
Green £100/$100
Punch Bowl Set
Marigold £3000/$3000; Amethyst £2000/$2000;
Green £2000/$2000
Spittoon
Marigold £7000/$7000

DIAMONDS
Manufactured by SWE   *Picture page 48*
aka DIAMANT

DIAMOND & SUNFLOWER
Manufactured by SWE
aka SOLROS
See also SUNFLOWER . . . SUNFLOWER & DIAMONDS
Vase
Marigold £65/$115; Blue £260+/$470

DIAMOND & WEDGES (MQB)
Manufactured by SWE   *Picture page 48, 81*
Bowl – Small
Marigold £85/$155; Blue £165/$300
Bowl – Large
Marigold £95/$170; Blue £225/$405

DIAMOND LACE
Manufactured in USA by Heisey   *Picture page 48*
Bowl 10"+
Marigold £45/$45; Amethyst £65/$65
Bowl 5"
Marigold £40/$40; Amethyst £60/$60
Pitcher
Amethyst £300/$300
Tumbler
Marigold £170/$170; Amethyst £65/$65

DIAMOND OVALS & BEADS (Ron May)
Manufactured by HRL   *Drawing by Ron May page 85*
Cake Plate on stem
Marigold £58/$105

DIAMOND PANES (MQB)
Manufactured by US   *Picture page 80*
Marigold £5/$5

DIAMOND POINTS
Manufactured by USF   *Picture page 81*
Vase
Marigold £30/$30; Amethyst £55/$55; Green £55/$55;
Pastel £160+/$160+

DIAMOND PRISMS
Manufactured in EUR   *Picture page 48*
Compote - Amber base
Marigold £30/$55; Amber £65/$115

DIAMOND SPEARS (Derek White)
Manufactured in EUR   *Drawing by Ron May page 85*
Bowl 9" approx
Marigold £28/$50

DIAMOND WEDGES
Manufactured in SWE   *Picture page 81*
Small bowl
Blue £165/$300

FLOWER SPRAY & DIAMONDS (MQB)
Manufactured by FRI   *Picture page 79*
Tumbler
Marigold £165/$300

FRILLS & DIAMONDS (Ron May)
Manufactured by USI   *Drawing by Ron May page 85*
Bowl 9"
Marigold £28/$28

HEAVY DIAMONDS FLOAT BOWL
Manufactured in Australia – one size   *Picture page 56*
Black Amethyst £285/$515

MITRED DIAMONDS & PLEATS
Manufactured by ESW   *Picture page 48*
Small Nappy
Marigold £28/$50

PANELLED (DIAMONDS)
Manufactured by AUS   *Picture page 63*
Sugar – 2 handles
Black Amethyst base £65/$115

PANELLED DIAMONDS
Manufactured by USF   *Picture page 80*
Tumbler
Amethyst £88/$88; Marigold £28/$28

STIPPLE DIAMOND SWAGS
See SWATHE & DIAMONDS

SUNFLOWER & DIAMONDS
Manufactured by SWE
See SUNFLOWER . . . SUNFLOWER & DIAMONDS
aka SOLROS (Sweden)

SWATHE & DIAMONDS
Manufactured in EUR   *Picture page 74*
Compote
Marigold £38/$70
Creamer
Marigold £28/$50

DIANA BOWL
Named in Australia   *Picture page 48*
Marigold £165/$300

DIVING DOLPHINS
Manufactured by ESB   *Picture page 49*
As exterior pattern
Amethyst £260+/$470; Marigold £100/$180
also internal pattern to SCROLL EMBOSS

DOGWOOD SPRAYS
Manufactured by USD   *Picture page 49*
Compote
Marigold £200/$200; Amethyst £250/$250;
Aqua Opal £300/$300

DOLPHINS
see DIVING DOLPHINS

DOUBLE DUTCH
Manufactured by USI
see WINDMILL (variant)

DOUBLE STEMMED ROSE
Manufactured by USD
See ROSE . . . TEXAS ROSE

DRAGON...

DRAGON & LOTUS
Manufactured by USF   *Picture page 49*
Bowl – 9" Flat Topaz**
Marigold £165/$165; Amethyst £195/$195;
Green £195/$195; Blue £195/$195; Peach Opal £350/$350;
Topaz £4000+/$4000
Bowl
Red £4000+/$4000
Bowl footed
Marigold £185/$185; Amethyst £215/$215;
Green £215/$215; Blue £215/$215; Peach Opal £215/$215
Plate 9"+
Marigold £2000/$2000

DRAGON & STRAWBERRY
Manufactured by USF   *Picture page 49*
Bowl flat 9"
Marigold £185/$185; Amethyst £800+/$800;
Green £500/$500; Blue £500/$500; Aqua Opal £2300/$2300
Bowl footed 9"
Marigold £300/$300; Green £800/$800; Blue £600+/$600

Plate (*aka Absentee Dragon*)
Marigold £3000+/$5400

DRAGON'S TONGUES
Manufactured by USF   *Picture page 49*
Lampshade **
Marigold £45/$45; Marigold on milk £165/$165

DRAPERY
Manufactured by USN   *Picture page 49*
Vase
Marigold £45/$45; Amethyst £165/$165; Green £85/$85;
Pastel £250/$250
Rose Bowl
Marigold £200/$200; Amethyst £95/$95; Green £95/$95;
Blue £105/$105
Candy Dish
Marigold £45/$45; Amethyst £85/$85; Green £120/$120;
Blue £80/$80

DREIBUS ADVERTISING DISH**
Picture page 49
Amethyst £500+/$900

DUCHESSE BASKET (Derek White)
Manufactured in EUR   *Drawing by Ron May on page 86*
Basket – plate shaped with arched handle
Marigold £48/$85

EDSTROM (Source)
aka STAR & HOBS
Manufactured by SWE   *Picture page 49*
Bowl – Extra large
Marigold £185/$335; Blue £325/$585
Banana Boat shape
Marigold £225/$405; Blue £425/$765

EGG & DART
Manufactured in EUR   *Picture page 49*
Candlestick – stubby
Marigold £15/$25

ELEPHANT MUG
Manufactured in USA   *Picture page 79*
Blue £58/$58

ELK...

ATLANTIC CITY ELK
Manufactured by USF   *Picture page 49, 50*
Bowl**
Blue £900/$900
Bowl – Two eyed elk
Amethyst £625/$625

EMU
Named in Australia   *Picture page 50*
Bowl – on Aqua
Marigold £380/$685
Compote – on clear
Marigold £360/$650

ENAMELLED CHERRIES
See CHERRY . . . ENAMELLED CHERRY

ENAMELLED CLEMATIS (MQB)
Manufactured in EUR   *Picture page 50*
Wine set
Marigold £850/$1550

ENAMELLED IRIS
See IRIS . . . ENAMELLED IRIS

ENGLISH HOB & BUTTON
Manufactured in ENG
See CHUNKY (MQB)
Bowl
Marigold £30/$55; Blue £60/$110
Cake plate – 2 tier with stand
Marigold £90/$160
Epergne – 2 bowl
Marigold £110/$200

ENGLISH HOBSTAR
Manufactured in ENG***   *Picture page 50*
Bowl and metal basket holding bowl
Marigold £85/$155

EROS
aka GOLDEN CUPID
Named in Australia

EUREKA FLAG
See chapter on Australian production

EUREKA FLORAL CROSS
See chapter on Australian production

FACET BAND (Ron May)
Manufactured in ENG   *Drawing by Ron May page 86*
Rose Bowl – small
Marigold £20/$35

FACETS (MQB)
Manufactured in ENG   *Picture page 50*
Bowl – large, legged
Marigold £85/$155

FAN/FANS...

FAN
Manufactured by USD   *Picture page 50*
Sauce Boat
Peach Opal £165/$165

FANS WATER SET
aka DOUBLE FANS   *Picture page 50*
Only known English Water Set to date
Marigold £1200/$2160
Pitcher
Marigold £180/$335
Tumbler
Marigold £150/$270

FANLIGHT DOUBLE CANDLESTICK (MQB)
Manufactured in EUR   *Picture page 58*
Marigold £65/$115; Green £95/$170

FANTAIL
Manufactured by USF   *Picture page 50*
Bowl 5" – footed
Marigold £45/$45; Blue £185/$185
Bowl 9" – footed **
Marigold £85/$85; Blue £220/$220
Compote
Marigold £70/$70; Blue £195/$195

Also see QUILTED FANS

FARMYARD
Manufactured by USD   *Picture page 50*
Bowl – 10"**
Amethyst £5000+/$5000; Green £8000+/$8000;
Peach Opal £10000+/$10000
Plate 10" (very rare)
Amethyst £1800+/$3240

FEATHER . . .

FEATHER & HEART
Manufactured by USM   *Picture page 51*
Pitcher**
Marigold £500+/$500; Amethyst £700+/$700;
Green £800+/$800

FEATHERS
Manufactured by USN   *Picture page 80*
Vase
Marigold £48/$45; Amethyst £85/$85; Green £95/$95;
Blue £105/$105

FENTONIA
Manufactured by USF   *Picture page 51*
Bowl – footed 9"+
Marigold £85/$85; Blue £135/$135
Bowl – footed 5"
Marigold £38/$38; Blue £48/$48
Bowl – fruit 10"
Marigold £65/$65; Amethyst £85/$85; Blue £95/$95
Butter
Marigold £100/$100; Blue £135/$135
Pitcher**
Marigold £500+/$500; Blue £700+/$700
Tumbler
Marigold £125/$125; Blue £200/$200

FERN . . .

FERN
Manufactured by USF   *Picture page 51*
Bowl 7"-9"
Manufactured by USN
Bowl – 6", 9"
Marigold £35/$35; Amethyst £45/$45; Green £45/$45
Compote
Marigold £45/$45; Amethyst £75/$75; Green £75/$75;
Blue £85/$85
Hat
Marigold £65/$65; Amethyst £95/$95; Green £105/$105

FIELD THISTLE
See ALEXANDER FLORAL

FILE
Manufactured by USI   *Picture page 51*
Exterior pattern
Bowl – small
Marigold £28/$28; Amethyst £45/$45

FILE
Manufactured by ESW – European variants   *Picture page 51*
Pin Bowl (exterior pattern):
with SOWERBY mark Marigold £38/$70

FINE BAND CELERY VASE
Manufactured in EUR   *Picture page 81*
Marigold £65/$115

FINE CUT OVALS
Manufactured by USM   *Picture page 51*
Exterior to WHIRLING LEAVES
This pattern also found in EUR
Bowl**
Marigold £75/$75; Amethyst £180/$180; Green £220/$220

FINE CUT RINGS
Manufactured by HRL   *Picture page 51*
Marigold £65/$115

FINE ETCHED FERN (MQB)
See FERN . . . FINE ETCHED FERN

FINE RIB COMPOTE
Manufactured by USN   *Picture page 79*
Marigold £38/$38; Green £48/$48

FIRCONE
Manufactured by USF   *Picture page 51*
Also see PINECONE
Bowl
Marigold £45/$45; Amethyst £65/$65

FIRCONES (MQB)
Manufactured by FRI   *Picture page 51*
Pitcher
Blue £1200/$2160
Tumbler
Blue £350/$630

FISH . . .

FISH BOWL
Manufactured in EUR   *Picture page 51*
Marigold £38/$70

FISHERMAN'S MUG
Manufactured in USA   *Picture page 78*
Marigold £190/$190; Amethyst £125/$125; Blue £450/$450;
Peach Opal £1450/$1450; Pastel £255/$255

LITTLE FISHES
Manufactured by USF   *Picture page 51*
Bowl – flat or footed 10"
Marigold £180/$180; Green £300/$300; Blue £350/$350
Bowl – flat or footed 5"+
Marigold £48/$48; Green £225/$225; Blue £225/$225;
Peach Opal £200/$200
Plate 10"+ (rare)
Blue £800+/$800

Also see TROUT AND FLY

FLOAT BOWL & FROG
Manufactured in Australia
See DIAMONDS . . . HEAVY DIAMONDS

FLORAL & GRAPE VARIANT**
Manufactured by USF   *Picture page 51*
Pitcher – 2 versions
Marigold £165/$165; Amethyst £225/$225; Blue £285/$285
Tumbler
Marigold £48/$48; Amethyst £98/$98; Blue £98/$98

FLORENTINE
Manufactured by USI   *Picture page 80*
Candlesticks – each
Marigold £85/$85

FLOWERS . . .

(ENAMELLED) FLOWERS
Manufactured by USF   *Picture page 52*
Bowl
Marigold £85/$85

FLOWERS & FRAMES
Manufactured by USD   *Picture page 52*
Bowl**
Marigold £35/$35; Amethyst £200/$200; Green £200/$200;
Peach Opal £265/$265

FLOWERSPRAY & DIAMONDS (MQB)
Picture page 79
Marigold £165/$300

(FORMAL) FLOWERS (MQB)
Picture page 52
Milk Jug
Marigold £35/$65

(FOUR) FLOWERS
Manufactured by USD and others USA &
VARIANTS Scandinavia.   *Picture page 52*
aka OHLSON (Sweden) and PODS & POSIES (USA)
Can have THUMBPRINTS exterior
Bowl – large Emerald base
Emerald Green £265/$265
Bowl – Eda, thin glass
Blue £825/$825
Bowl – yellow base
Pastel £650/$650
Dugan USA
Peach Opal £125/$125
Eda Sweden – Bowl
Pastel £550/$550

(LITTLE) FLOWERS
Manufactured by USF   *Picture page 52*
Bowl 9"+
Marigold £75/$75; Amethyst £95/$95; Green £100/$100;
Blue £100/$100; Red £10000+/$10000
Bowl 5"+
Marigold £45/$45; Amethyst £80/$80; Green £70/$70;
Blue £80/$80
Plate 7" (rare)
Marigold £180/$180
Plate 10" (extremely rare)
Marigold £600/$600

(TWO) FLOWERS
Manufactured by USF   *Picture page 52*
Plate 13"
Marigold £3000+/$3000
Bowl footed
Marigold £48/$48; Amethyst £68/$68; Green £68/$68;
Blue £68/$68
Plate footed
Marigold £600+/$600; Green £650/$650; Blue £650/$650

FOOTED PRISMS
Manufactured by ESW   *Picture page 52*
Vase
Marigold £185/$335; Blue £325/$585

FORTY-FIVE (Ron May)
Manufactured in EUR   *Drawing by Ron May page 86*
Bowl – shallow, stubby feet
Marigold £28/$50

FOUR CROWNS (MQB)
Manufactured by FRI   *Picture page 78*
aka PINEAPPLE CROWN
Plate
Marigold £165/$300

FOUR-SEVEN-FOUR
Manufactured by USI   *Picture page 53, 81*
Pitcher
Marigold £180/$180; Amethyst £400/$400;
Green £350/$350; Pastel £500+/$500
Tumbler
Marigold £40/$40; Amethyst £120/$120; Green £100/$100

FOUR SIDED TREE TRUNK VASE (MQB)
Picture page 53
Marigold £88/$160

FREEHAND (MQB)
Manufactured in ENG   *Picture page 53*
Modern
Blue £85/$155
_____

FRILLS & DIAMONDS (Ron May)
Manufactured in ENG
See DIAMOND . . . FRILLS & DIAMONDS
_____

FROLICKING BEARS CUSPIDOR
See (FROLICKING) BEARS
USA Souvenir new issue
Red Base colour £125/$125
_____

FROSTED BLOCK
Manufactured by USI   *Picture page 53*
Bowl – 6"
Marigold £35/$35; Clear £45/$45
Butter
Marigold £40/$40; Clear £60/$60
Sugar/Creamer
Marigold £40/$40; Clear £70/$70
Rose Bowl
Marigold £45/$45; Clear £90/$90
Compote
Marigold £60/$60; Clear £60/$60
Pickle Dish
Marigold £45/$45
_____

FRUITS . . .

FRUITS & FLOWERS
Variant of THREE FRUITS
Manufactured by USN   *Picture page 53*
Bon Bon
Marigold £75/$75; Amethyst £95/$95; Green £95/$95;
Blue £125/$125; Aqua Opal £400/$400 _ _ _ _ _ _ _ _ _ _

MANY FRUITS
Manufactured by USD _ _ _ _ _ _ _ _ _ _ _ _ _ _ _ _ _ _

THREE FRUITS
Manufactured by USN   *Picture page 75*
Bowl 9"
Marigold £85/$85; Amethyst £125/$125;
Green £125/$125; Blue £145/$145; Aqua Opal £800+/$800
Bowl 5"
Marigold £28/$28; Amethyst £45/$45; Green £45/$45;
Blue £50/$50
Bon-Bon
Marigold £40/$40; Amethyst £60/$60; Green £65/$65;
Blue £75/$75; Aqua Opal £800+/$800 _ _ _ _ _ _ _ _ _ _

TWO FRUITS
Manufactured by USF   *Picture page 53*
Bowl – divided – scarce
Marigold £75/$75; Amethyst £95/$95; Green £165/$165;
Blue £165/$165
_____

GARDEN PATH
Manufactured by USD and FRI   *Picture page 53*
Bowl Interior on Rio glass £85/$85
_____

GARLAND
aka DAINTY GOBLET*
Manufactured by USF   *Picture page 53*
Compote on legs
Marigold £65/$65; Amethyst £85/$85; Green £85/$85;
Blue £85/$85
Manufactured by Indiana USA
Repro ware piece
Blue £125/$125

GEOMETRICS (MQB)
Manufactured in ENG?
See KOKOMO
_____

GLADER
Named in Sweden (SWE)   *Picture page 53*
aka STAR & FAN (MQB)
Banana Boat shape
Marigold £65/$115; Blue £165/$300
_____

GODDESS OF THE HARVEST
Manufactured by USF   *Picture page 53*
Bowl 9"+**
Amethyst £3835/$3835
Plate
Amethyst £3890/$3890
_____

GOLDEN CUPID
Manufactured in Australia
_____

GOLDEN HARVEST DECANTER
Manufactured by USI   *Picture page 53*
Marigold £90/$90; Amethyst £150/$150
_____

GOLDEN THISTLE
See THISTLE . . . GOLDEN THISTLE
_____

GOOD LUCK
Manufactured by USN   *Picture page 53*
And with Variant. And with STIPPLE RAYS exterior
Bowl 8"+
Marigold £200/$200; Amethyst £300/$300;
Green £350/$350; Blue £400/$400
Plate 9"
Marigold £350+/$350; Amethyst £600+/$600;
Green £700+/$700; Blue £900+/$900
Variant Bowl 8"+
Marigold £250+/$250; Amethyst £350+/$350;
Green £400+/$400
_____

GOTHIC ARCHES
Manufactured by USF
aka GRAPE & GOTHIC ARCHES
_____

GRAND THISTLE
Manufactured by FRI
aka WIDE PANELLED THISTLE
Also see ALEXANDER FLORAL
_____

GRAPE . . .

CENTRAL GRAPE & LEAVES
Manufactured in ENG
Bowl
Marigold £28/$50 _ _ _ _ _ _ _ _ _ _ _ _ _ _ _ _ _ _ _

GRAPE & GOTHIC ARCHES
Manufactured by USN
Creamer/Sugar
Manufactured by USF   *Picture page 82*
Tumbler
Marigold £38/$38; Amethyst £80/$80; Green £80/$80;
Blue £90/$90 _

GRAPE & CABLE
Manufactured by USN   *Picture page 53, 54, 78, 82*
Fernery – rare
Marigold £850/$850; Amethyst £70/$70;
Green £750/$750; White £1000+/$1000
Butter & Lid
Marigold £175/$175; Amethyst £220/$220
Bowl 10"
Marigold £150/$150; Amethyst £75/$75; Green £80/$80;
Blue £80/$80; Aqua Opal £3000+/$3000

Nappy
Marigold £75/$75; Amethyst £95/$95; Green £125/$125;
Blue £185/$185
Pitcher
Marigold £225/$225; Amethyst £250/$250;
Green £275/$275
Tumbler
Marigold £38/$38; Amethyst £48/$48; Green £48/$48;
Blue £48/$48
Punch Set
Marigold £280/$280; Amethyst £400/$400;
Green £400/$400; Blue £900/$900
Punch Cup
Marigold £28/$28; Amethyst £48/$48; Green £48/$48;
Blue £60/$60

GRAPE & FLOWER
Manufactured by USF and USD   *Picture page 82*
aka BANDED FLORAL & GRAPE
Marigold £38/$38; Amethyst £78/$78; Blue £78/$78

GRAPE ARBOR
Manufactured by USD   *Picture page 54, 81*
Marigold £65/$65; Amethyst £85/$85; Blue £250/$250

GRAPEVINE LATTICE
Manufactured by USF   *Picture page 54*
Pitcher
Tumbler
Manufactured by USD
Bowl – shallow
Marigold £35/$35; Amethyst £45/$45; Green £45/$45;
Blue £45/$45; White £80/$80
Plate
Marigold £200/$200; Amethyst £200/$200; Blue £200/$200;
White £250/$250
Hat Shape
Marigold £60/$60

HEAVY GRAPE
Manufactured by USI   *Picture page 54, 82*
Plate 6" plate
Marigold £70/$70; Amethyst £185/$185; Green £85/$85
Bowl 9"
Marigold £45/$45; Amethyst £65/$655; Green £65/$65
Punch bowl and top
Marigold £125/$125; Amethyst £350/$350;
Green £300/$300
Wine Goblet
Marigold £38/$38; Amethyst £48/$48; Green £48/$48

HELIOS GRAPE
Manufactured by USI
Bowl
Green £65/$65

IMPERIAL GRAPE
Manufactured by USI   *Picture page 54*
Bowl
Marigold £30/$30; Amethyst £40/$40; Green £40/$40
Punch Set
Marigold £125/$125; Amethyst £350/$350;
Green £300/$300
Decanter – Repro 1970s
Marigold £38/$38; Amethyst £48/$48

LOTUS & GRAPE
See LOTUS & GRAPE

PEACOCK & GRAPE
See PEACOCK & GRAPE

VINTAGE
Manufactured by USD   *Picture page 54*
Powder Bowl & Lid
Marigold £58/$58; Amethyst £100/$100; Blue £130/$130
Rose bowl
Marigold £45/$45; Amethyst £65/$65; Green £55/$55;
Blue £55/$55
Manufactured by USF
Epergne
Marigold £85/$85; Amethyst £100/$100;
Green £120/$120; Blue £120/$120
Fernery
Marigold £38/$38; Amethyst £55/$55; Green £75/$75;
Blue £65/$65
Bowls 8", 10"
Marigold £38/$38; Amethyst £48/$48; Green £55/$55;
Blue £65/$65; Red £2000+/$2000
Plate
Marigold £200+/$200; Amethyst £400+/$400;
Green £200+/$200; Blue £100+/$100
Rose Bowl
Marigold £35/$35; Blue £55/$55
Manufactured by USM   *Picture page 54*
Bowl – 5" Extremly rare
Bowl – 9" Extremly rare

GRAVEYARD SPHERE (MQB)
Manufactured by SWE   *Picture page 54*
No price available

GREEK KEY. . .

GREEK KEY
Manufactured by USN   *Picture page 54*
Bowl
Marigold £180/$180; Amethyst £80/$80; Green £90/$90;
Blue £250/$250

GREEK KEY & SCALES
Manufactured in the USA   *Picture page 54*
External pattern
Marigold £60/$60; Amethyst £80/$85; Green £80/$80

GREEK KEY & SUNBURST VASE
Possibly Dutch   *Picture page 55*
Marigold £68/$120

GRETA (MQB)
Manufactured by HRL   *Picture page 55*
Milk Jug
Marigold £28/$50

HAMBURG
Manufactured by SWE. Named in Sweden (source)
aka RANDEL VARIANT   *Picture page 55, 38*
Bowl
Marigold £185/$335; Blue £425/$765

HAND VASE
Czechoslovakian?   *Picture page 55, 81*
With Watch
Marigold £85/$155
Vase on Green Iridised acid etched Camphor glass
Green (on Camphor) £385/$695; Yellow base £85/$155

HANS (MQB)
Possibly manufactured by HRL   *Picture page 55*
Compote – small
Marigold £38/$70

HATTIE
Manufactured by USI   *Picture page 55*
aka BUSY LIZZIE
Bowl
Marigold £35/$35; Amethyst £85/$85
Rose Bowl
Marigold £80/$80; Pastel – amber £180/$180
Plate – rare
Marigold £750+/$750; Amethyst £900+/$900

HAZEL (MQB)
Found at SWE (n/k if made at Eda)   *Picture page 55*
Vase
Marigold £65/$115

HEADDRESS
Interior pattern to CURVED STAR   *Picture page 55*
Compote
Marigold £45/$80; Blue £85/$155

HEART/HEARTS. . .

HEARTS & FLOWERS
Manufactured by USN   *Picture page 55, 56*
Compote**
Marigold £200/$200; Amethyst £375/$375;
Green £1500+/$1500; Blue £375/$375;
Pastel (Ice Blue) £2000/$2000; Ice Green £2000/$2000
Bowl 8"
Marigold £430/$430; Amethyst £230/$230;
Green £650/$650; Blue £550/$550;
Aqua Opal £700/$700; Pastel (Ice Blue) £800/$800
Plate 9"
Marigold £800+/$800; Amethyst £950+/$950;
Green £2500/$2500; Blue £450/$450; Aqua Opal £2000/$2000

HEARTS & HORSESHOES
Manufactured by USF   *Picture page 56*
Bowl 8"+
Marigold £750/$750; Green £850/$850
Plate 9" rare
Marigold £100/$100; Green £850/$850

HEARTS & TREES
Manufactured by USF   *Picture page 56*
Internal pattern with BUTTERFLY & BERRY
Master Bowl**
Marigold £135/$135

HEART & VINE
Manufactured by USF   *Picture page 56*
Bowl
Marigold £65/$65; Amethyst £98/$98; Green £78/$78;
Blue £98/$98
Plate**
Marigold £250/$250; Amethyst £350/$350;
Green £265/$265; Blue £480/$480

(JEWELLED) HEART
Manufactured by USD   *Picture page 56*
aka LATTICE & HEART
Bowl 5"
Amethyst £40/$40; Peach Opal £85/$85
Bowl 10"
Amethyst £75/$75; Peach Opal £105/$105
Pitcher
Marigold £800/$800
Tumbler
Marigold £80/$80
Plate 6"
Marigold £175/$175; Peach Opal £185/$185
Whimsey (Amethyst) £565/$565
turned up tulip edge all round on exterior pattern

(STREAM OF) HEARTS
Manufactured by USF   *Picture page 56*
Bowl 10" footed
Goblet
Marigold £150/$150
Compote
With Persian Medallion** interior
Marigold £220/$220

HEAVY CUT (MQB)
Manufactured by FRI   *Picture page 56*
Banana Boat shape
Marigold £85/$155

HEAVY DIAMONDS
Australian
See DIAMONDS . . . HEAVY DIAMONDS

HEN
Manufactured by ESW
See . . . COVERED HEN

HERRINGBONE & IRIS
Manufactured in USA by Jeanette   *Picture page 56*
Pitcher
Marigold £125/$125
Tumbler
Marigold £65/$65

HOBNAIL . . .

HOBNAIL
Manufactured by USM   *Picture page 64*
Pitcher
Marigold £1500/$1500; Amethyst £1600/$1600;
Green £1800/$1800 Blue £1200/$1200
Tumbler
Marigold £650/$650; Amethyst £350/$350;
Green £850/$850; Blue £750/$750
Rose Bowl
Marigold £125/$125; Amethyst £350/$350; Green £450/$450
Spittoon
Marigold £750/$750; Amethyst £850/$850;
Green £1300/$1300
Butter – rare
Marigold £400/$400; Amethyst £500/$500;
Green £525/$525; Blue £70/$700
Creamer/Sugar
Marigold £210/$210; Amethyst £310/$310;
Green £410/$410; Blue £480/$480

HOBNAIL BANDED TUMBLERS
Manufactured by EMK rare   *Picture page 56*
Marigold £680/$1225; Blue £800/$1440

SWIRLED HOBNAIL
Manufactured by USM   *Picture page 56*
Rose Bowl**
Marigold £225/$225; Amethyst £285/$285;
Green £480/$480

HOBSTAR. . .

HOBSTAR & CUT TRIANGLES
Manufactured by ESW   *Picture page 57*
Bowl
Marigold £30/$55; Amethyst £75/$135
Rose Bowl
Marigold £30/$55; Amethyst £40/$70; Green £50/$90
Plate
Marigold £50/$90; Amethyst £85/$155; Green £95/$170

HOBSTAR & FEATHER
Manufactured by USM   *Picture page 56*
Punch Bowl set
Marigold £1500/$1500; Green £3500+/$3500
Punch Cup
Marigold £30/$30; Amethyst £40/$40
Rose Bowl Giant size 8½"
Marigold £3000/$3000; Amethyst £2000/$2000;
Green £2000/$2000
Compote 6" rare
Marigold £1400/$1400

- -

HOBSTAR & TASSELS
Manufactured by USI   *Picture page 57*
Bowl
Amethyst £155/$155

- -

HOBSTAR FLOWERS
Manufactured by USN   *Picture page 57*
Compote – scarce
Marigold £145/$145; Amethyst £150/$150;
Green £250/$250; Blue £260/$260

HOBSTAR
See also LONG HOBSTAR

HOLLY . . .

CARNIVAL HOLLY
Manufactured by USF   *Picture page 57*
aka HOLLY
Bowl
Marigold £45/$45; Amethyst £85/$85; Green £165/$165;
Blue £85/$85; Red £2000/$2000
Compote 5"
Marigold £35/$35; Amethyst £85/$85; Green £185/$185;
Blue £50/$50
Hat
Marigold £35/$35; Amethyst £48/$48; Green £95/$95;
Blue £90/$90; Red £600/$600
Goblet
Marigold £35/$65; Amethyst £45/$80; Green £95/$170;
Blue £210/$210; Red £1000+/$1000
Plate 9"
Marigold £210/$210; Amethyst £600+/$600;
Green £1000+/$1000; Blue £280/$280; Red £2400+/$2400

HOLLY & BERRY
Manufactured by USD   *Picture page 57*
Bowl
Marigold £60/$60; Amethyst £70/$70; Green £90/$90;
Blue £80/$80; Red £2000+/$2000; White £100/$100
Nappy
Marigold £40/$40; Amethyst £50/$50; Green £55/$55;
Blue £60/$60; Peach Opal £70/$70
Sauce Boat – one handle
Amethyst £65/$65; Blue £65/$65; Peach Opal £140/$140

HOLLY SPRIG
Picture page 57
Hat
Marigold £35/$65; Amethyst £40/$70; Green £125/$225;
Blue £120/$215; Red £750/$1350

HONEYCOMBE & CLOVER
Exterior pattern to FEATHERED SERPENT   *Picture page 57*
Marigold £85/$155; Amethyst £125/$225;
Green £100/$180; Blue £125/$225

HORSES
Manufactured by USF   *Picture page 57*
aka HORSES HEADS or HORSES MEDALLIONS
Also see PONY
Footed Bowl
Marigold £125/$125; Green £300/$300; Blue £210/$210;
Red £900/$900; White £220/$220

IDYLL VASE**
Manufactured by USF   *Picture page 57*
Waterlily & Cattail pattern
Marigold £450/$450; Amethyst £600+/$600;
Blue £700+/$700

ILLUSION
Manufactured by USF   *Picture page 57*
Bon Bon
Marigold £38/$38; Blue £78/$78
Bowl
Marigold £30/$30; Blue £68/$68

INGA VASE (MQB)
Manufactured in SWE   *Picture page 57*
Marigold £85/$155

INTAGLIO STRAWBERRY
See STRAWBERRY . . . (INTAGLIO) STRAWBERRY

INVERTED BLOCKS
Manufactured in EUR   *Picture page 81, 82*
Marigold £45/$80

IRIS . . .

ENAMELLED IRIS
Picture page 80
Tumbler
Marigold £78/$140; Green £125/$225; Blue £165/$300

HERRINGBONE & IRIS
Manufactured in USA by Jeanette
Depression ware water set
Pitcher
Marigold on clear £125/$125
Tumbler
Marigold on clear £65/$65 each

- -

IRIS
Manufactured by USF   *Picture page 57*
Compote on stem
Marigold £38/$38; Amethyst £48/$48; Green £48/$48;
Blue £48/$48; White £180/$180

JACK-IN-THE-PULPIT
Manufactured in Europe   *Picture page 81*
Marigold £40/$70; Amethyst £60/$110; Blue £60/$110;
Peach Opal £78/$140

JET BLACK BEAUTY (MQB)
Manufactured by FRI   *Picture page 58*
Plate – two open handles
Jet £1650/$2970

JETTA VASE (MQB)
Scandinavian or European   *Picture page 58*
Jet £650/$1170

JEWELLED HEART
See HEART.. JEWELLED HEART

JULIANA VASE (MQB)
Manufactured by EMK   *Picture page 58*
Blue £450/$810

KANGAROO
Named in Australia   *Picture page 58*
Bowl – small
Marigold £165/$300; Black Amethyst £265/$480
Bowl – large
Black Amethyst £325/$585

KAREN (MQB)
Manufactured by SWE   *Picture page 58*
Bowl – deep
Green (pale) £185/$335

KINGFISHER
Named in Australia   *Picture page 58*
Bowl
Marigold £175/$315
Bowl
Black Amethyst £325/$585

KITTENS
Manufactured by USF   *Picture page 58*
Bowl – 4" Scarce
Blue £700+/$700
Cup and Saucer
Marigold £180/$180
Spooner 2"+
Marigold £125/$125
Plate 4"+
Marigold £125/$125; Blue £400+/$400
Vase 3"
Marigold £125/$125

KIWI
Named in Australia   *Picture page 58*
With SCROLL & DAISY as exterior pattern
Compote – small
Marigold £225/$405; Black Amethyst £325/$585

KNOTTED BEADS
Manufactured by USF   *Picture page 80*
Vase scarce in UK
Marigold £38/$38; Green £68/$68; Blue £68/$68

KOHINOOR
European manufacture   *Picture page 58*
aka BEVELLED DIAMONDS & RAYS (A Hallam)
Bowl – shallow
Marigold £30/$55

KOKOMO
European manufacture   *Picture page 58*
aka GEOMETRICS
Bowl – 3 footed
Marigold £35/$65; Amethyst £55/$100

KOOKABURRA
Australian manufacture   *Picture page 58*
Bowl 5"
Marigold £165/$300; Black Amethyst £265/$480
Bowl 9"
Marigold £225/$405; Black Amethyst £325/$585

KULOR (Source)
Manufactured by SWE   *Picture page 58*
aka MOONPRINT & INVERTED THUMBPRINTS (USA/UK)
Vase
Marigold £165/$300; Blue £265/$480;
Milk Glass £1000/$1800
Bowl
Marigold £165/$300; Blue £265/$480
Muffin Dish and Lid
Marigold £185/$335; Blue £285/$515

Butter and Lid
Marigold £185/$335; Blue £285/$515
Compote
Marigold £165/$300; Blue £265/$480
Creamer/Sugar

LAGERKRANTZ
Manufactured by SWE (ex-catalogue Source)   *Picture page 59*
Bonbonniere
Marigold £650/$1170; Blue £850/$1550

LASSE (Source)
See CURVED STAR alternative name

LATTICE & GRAPE
Manufactured by USF   *Picture page 59*
Pitcher**
Marigold £220/$220; Amethyst £385/$385;
Green £425/$425; Blue £325/$325;
Peach Opal £2000+/$2000; White £800+/$800
Tumbler**
Marigold £65/$65; Amethyst £85/$85;
Green £85/$85; Blue £95/$95;
Peach Opal £500/$500; White £200+/$200

LAUREL WREATH (Ron May)
Manufactured in EUR   *Drawing by Ron May page 86*
Compote – stemmed
Marigold £48/$85

LEAF . . .

LEAF & BEADS
Manufactured by USN and USD   *Picture page 59*
Plate Whimsey
Marigold £210/$210; Amethyst £220/$220;
Green £500+/$500; Aqua Opal £200+/$200;
Pastel £400/$400
Candy Dish Footed
Marigold £65/$65; Amethyst £85/$85; Green £95/$95
Rose Bowl on Legs
Marigold £65/$65; Amethyst £85/$85; Green £95/$95;
Aqua Opal £400+/$400
Bowl – Nut
sometimes with patterned interior – adds approx 20% value

LEAF CHAIN
Manufactured by USF   *Picture page 59*
Bowl
Marigold £48/$48; Amethyst £65/$65; Green £65/$65;
Blue £75/$75; Aqua Opal £1000+/$1000; Pastel £100/$100;
Red £1000+/$1000
Bon Bon
Marigold £48/$48; Amethyst £55/$55; Green £55/$55;
Blue £65/$65
Plate
Marigold £38/$38; Amethyst £100/$100; Green £120/$120;
Blue £90/$90; Aqua Opal £2000+/$2000; White £220/$220

LEAF TIERS
Picture page 80
Vase
Amethyst £65/$115

LEAFY TRIANGLE (Ron May)
Drawing by Ron May page 87
Bowl – shallow
Marigold £48/$85

LILY OF THE VALLEY
Manufactured by USF   *Picture page 59*
Water Pitcher**
Blue £4000+/$4000

Tumbler
Marigold £600/$1100; Blue £200/$360

LION
Manufactured by USF   *Picture page 59*
with BERRY & LEAF CIRCLE as exterior pattern
Bowl 7"
Marigold £125/$125; Blue £300/$300
Plate 7"+
Marigold £1000+/$1000

LITTLE FISHES
See FISH . . . LITTLE FISHES

LITTLE FLOWERS
See FLOWERS . . . LITTLE FLOWERS

LONDON
Named in Sweden (SWE)   *Picture page 59*
aka QUILLS & PANELS (MQB)
Bowl
Marigold £165/$300

LONG HOBSTAR
Manufactured by USI   *Picture page 59*
Also see HOBSTAR pattern
Punch Bowl Top Base
Marigold £150/$150

LONG THUMBPRINT
Manufactured by USD   *Picture page 80*
Vase
Green £28/$28

LOTUS . . .

LOTUS & DRAGON
See DRAGON & LOTUS

LOTUS & GRAPE
Manufactured by USF   *Picture page 59*
Bon Bon
Marigold £100/$100; Amethyst £125/$125;
Green £135/$135; Blue £130/$130; Red £800+/$800
Aqua £180/$180
Absentee Bowl – rare
Blue £1500+/$1500
Bowl – flat 7"
Marigold £40/$40; Amethyst £48/$48; Green £48/$48;
Blue £68/$68
Bowl footed 7"
Marigold £48/$48; Amethyst £55/$55; Green £55/$55;
Blue £68/$68
Plate 9" rare
Marigold £260/$260; Amethyst £2200+/$2200;
Green £1800+/$1800; Blue £1800+/$1800

LOUISA
Part of USA Jeanette Floragold range   *Picture page 59*
Tumbler
Marigold £38/$38
Ash Tray
Marigold £35/$35
Pitcher
Marigold £125/$125
Manufactured by Westmoreland USA

LOVING CUP
See MARY ANN VASE
Manufactured by USF
Orange Tree Loving Cup
Marigold £220/$220; Amethyst £400/$400;
Green £500/$500; Blue £500/$500;
Aqua Opal £5000+/$5000

MAGDA CANDLESTICK (MQB)
Manufactured by FRI   *Picture page 59*
Pastel (Ice Blue) £480/$850

MAGPIE (Australian)
See CROW

MANY FRUITS
Manufactured by USD   *Picture page 81*
Punch Cup
Marigold £28/$28; Amethyst £35/$35; Green £35/$35;
Blue £40/$40

MANY STARS
Manufactured by USM
See STARS . . . MANY STARS

MAPLE LEAF
Manufactured by USD   *Picture page 60*
Bowl stemmed 4"+
Marigold £38/$38; Amethyst £48/$48; Green £48/$48;
Blue £48/$48
Butter
Marigold £95/$95; Amethyst £105/$105; Blue £105/$105
Sugar/Creamer
Marigold £38/$38; Amethyst £48/$48; Blue £48/$48
Pitcher
Marigold £160/$160; Amethyst £265/$265; Blue £200/$200
Tumbler
Marigold £28/$28; Amethyst £48/$48; Blue £48/$48

MARBLES
Picture page 69
On bone marble holder (complete) £285/$515

MARILYN
Manufactured by USM   *Picture page 60*
Pitcher**
Marigold £750/$750; Amethyst £1000+/$1000;
Green £1300+/$1300

MARTHA
Manufactured by ENG   *Picture page 60*
Compote 7"+
Marigold £38/$70

MARY ANN VASE
Manufactured by USD   *Picture page 60*
See under LOVING CUPS for 3 handled version
Marigold £100/$100; Amethyst £250/$250

MATCHBOX HOLDER
Manufactured by FRI   *Picture page 60*
Marigold £65/$115

MAUD
Manufactured by SWE (ex-1930s catalogue)
Picture page 60
Bowl – shallow
Marigold £165/$300; Blue £265/$480

MAYAN
Manufactured by USM   *Picture page 60*
Bowl – shallow
Green £165/$165

MEMPHIS
Manufactured by USN   *Picture page 60, 82*
Bowl 10"
Marigold £80/$80; Amethyst £300+/$300; Green £175/$175
Bowl 5"
Marigold £28/$28; Amethyst £38/$38; Green £38/$38
Punch Bowl set
Marigold £300/$300; Amethyst £500/$500;
Green £575/$575

Punch Cup
Marigold £35/$65; Amethyst £48/$85; Green £48/$85

MEYDAM (MQB)
Manufactured by HRL   *Picture page 60*
Cake Plate on stem
Marigold £68/$120
Compote on stem
Marigold £38/$70
Butter
Marigold £48/$85
Sugar/Creamer
Marigold £28/$50

MIKADO
Manufactured by USF   *Picture page 60*
Massive Cherry Compote
Marigold £250/$250; Amethyst £1000+/$1000;
Green £1750+/$1750; Blue £300/$300;
Pastel (White) £600+/$600; Red £600+/$600
MILADY WATER SET
Manufactured by USF   *Picture page 60*
Water Pitcher**
Marigold £350/$350; Amethyst £550/$550;
Green £680/$680; Blue £825/$825
Tumbler**
Marigold £90/$90; Amethyst £110/$110;
Green £120/$120; Blue £130/$130

MITRED DIAMONDS & PLEATS
See DIAMONDS . . . MITRED DIAMONDS & PLEATS
Picture page 60
Bowl
Marigold £25/$45
Pin Dish
Marigold £38/$70

MOLLER
Manufactured by SWE (ex catalogue)   *Picture page 61*
Bowl – large
Marigold £185/$335; Blue £325/$585

MONEY BOXES
See OWL MONEY BOX

MOONPRINT
Manufactured by ENG/SWE/HRL/USA   *Picture page 61*
Bowl – large 10"+***
Marigold £48/$48
Creamer/Sugar
Marigold £28/$28

MORNING GLORY
Manufactured by USM   *Picture page 61*
Pitcher**
Marigold £8000+/$8000; Amethyst £8000+/$8000;
Green £9000+/$9000
Tumbler**
Marigold £900/$900; Amethyst £900+/$900;
Green £900+/$900

MY LADY POWDER BOWL
Possibly manufactured by Davisons England   *Picture page 61*
Marigold £80/$145

NANNA (Source)
Manufactured by SWE (ex catalogue)   *See page 61*
Vase
Marigold £165/$300

NANTIA (MQB)
Manufactured by SWE (ex catalogue)   *Picture page 61*
Plate
Marigold £265/$480; Blue £465/$840

NAUTILUS
Manufactured by USD using old Northwood mould
Picture page 61
Marigold £250/$250; Amethyst £280/$280;
Peach Opal £350/$350

NESTING SWAN
See SWAN . . . NESTING SWAN

NIPPON
Manufactured by USN   *Picture page 61*
With PEACOCKS TAILS as interior pattern
Bowl 8"+
Marigold £180/$180; Amethyst £220/$220;
Green £220/$220; Blue £220/$220; White £300/$300
Plate 9"
Marigold £300/$300; Amethyst £450/$450;
Green £550/$550; Blue £600/$600; White £1000+/$1000

NORA VASE (MQB)
Manufactured by EMK   *Picture page 61*
Marigold £68/$120; Blue £270/$485

NORTHERN LIGHTS
See STAR & HOBS . . . NORTHERN LIGHTS

NUTMEG GRATER
Manufactured by SWE   *Picture page 61*
Bowl
Marigold £85/$155
Compote – stemmed
Marigold £38/$70
Butter – covered
Marigold £68/$120
Manufactured by ESW
Sugar/Creamer
Marigold £28/$50

OBSIDIAN (MQB)
Possibly manufactured in EUR   *Picture page 45*
Candlestick (pair)
Jet base £260/$470 pair

OCTET
Manufactured by USN   *Picture page 87*
With exterior pattern NORTHWOOD VINTAGE
Bowl
Marigold £85/$85; Amethyst £110/$110; White £160/$160

OHLSON (Source)
See FLOWERS . . . FOUR FLOWERS

OIL LAMP
see OPAL ROCCOCO WAVES

OLGA (MQB)
Manufactured by SWE   *Picture page 61*
Bowl
Marigold £65/$115; Blue £165/$300

OLIVIA (MQB)
Possibly Val St Lambert, often seen in Belgium *Picture page 62*
aka COLUMBIA in USA
Giant Bowl - open edged, 12"+
Marigold £165/$165

OPAL ROCCOCO WAVES OIL LAMP (Frank Horn)
Manufactured in USA   *Picture page 67*
See ROCCOCO WAVES
Lilac £585/$585

OPEN EDGE BASKETWEAVE
Manufactured by USF   *Picture page 62*
Group Bowls – 5"
Marigold £48/$48; Amethyst £58/$58; Green £58/$58;
Blue £58/$58; Ice Green £220/$220
Bowl – Ice Blue, shallow 8"
Marigold £68/$68; Amethyst £88/$88; Green £88/$88;
Blue £88/$88; Ice Blue £250/$250
Bowl – 5"
Ice Blue £220/$220
Bowl – 8"
Ice Green £280/$280

OPEN ROSE
See ROSE . . . OPEN ROSE

ORANGE TREE. . .

ORANGE TREE
Manufactured by USF   *Picture page 62, 80, 82*
Hatpin Holder
Marigold £350/$350; Green £380/$380; Blue £380/$380;
Pastel (White) £400/$400
Bowl – flat, 8", 10"
Marigold £45/$45; Green £275/$275; Blue £125/$125
Bowl – footed 9", 11"
Marigold £105/$105; Green £115/$115; Blue £115/$115
Ice cream – small, stemmed
Marigold £25/$25; Blue £35/$35
Powder Jar and lid
Marigold £125/$125; Green £400/$400; Blue £165/$165
Loving Cup
See also under LOVING CUP
Marigold £200/$200; Amethyst £375/$375;
Green £450/$450; Blue £450/$450;
Peach Opal £4000+/$4000; Aqua Opal £5000+/$5000;
Pastel (White) £400/$400
Punch set – top and base
Marigold £130/$130; Amethyst £200/$200;
Green £200/$200; Blue £200/$200
Punch Cup
Marigold £28/$28; Green £38/$38; Blue £38/$38
Goblet – large
Marigold £75/$75
Wine
Marigold £38/$38; Blue £58/$58
Sugar/Creamer
Marigold £28/$28; Blue £48/$48
Butter
Marigold £300/$300; Blue £275/$275
Pitcher
Marigold £185/$185; Blue £265/$265
Tumbler
Marigold £35/$35; Blue £48/$48

ORANGE TREE ORCHARD
Manufactured by USF   *Picture page 62*
Pitcher**
Marigold £300/$300; Amethyst £400/$400;
Green £400/$400; Blue £450/$450
Tumbler
Marigold £48/$48; Amethyst £105/$105;
Green £105/$105; Blue £105/$105

ORANGE TREE VARIANT
Manufactured by USF   *Picture page 62*
Pitcher**
Blue £400+/$400
Tumbler**
Blue £150/$150

ORBIT (Ron May)
Manufactured in EUR   *Drawing by Ron May page 87*
Cake Plate – stemmed
Marigold £58/$105

ORCHID
See WISHBONE (Variant)

OREBRO
Manufactured by SWE   Drawing by John Masters page 38
aka NORTHERN LIGHTS
See STAR & HOBS (alternative name)

ORIENTAL (MQB)
Far East Reproduction Carnival Glass   *Picture page 62*
Ginger Jar and Box
Marigold £38/$70

ORIGAMI (Ron May)
Manufactured in EUR   *Drawing by Ron May page 87*
Fruit Bowl – shallow
Marigold £18/$35

ORNATE BEADS (MQB)
Manufactured by FDK   *Picture page 62*
Candlesticks (pair)
Blue £860/$1550

OSTRICH
Manufactured in Australia
See EMU

OWL MONEY BOX
Picture page 70
Marigold £45/$80

PALM BEACH
Manufactured by USD   *Picture page 62*
Rose Bowl
Marigold £28/$28; Amethyst £48/$48

PANELLED DANDELION
Manufactured by USF   *Picture page 62*
Pitcher
Marigold £400/$400; Amethyst £600/$600;
Green £70/$70; Blue £70/$70
Tumbler
Marigold £48/$48; Amethyst £85/$85; Green £85/$85;
Blue £95/$95

PANELLED DIAMONDS SUGAR
See DIAMONDS . . . PANELLED DIAMONDS SUGAR

PANELLED THISTLE
Manufactured by FRI
See ALEXANDER FLORAL

PANELS & THUMBPRINTS
See THUMBPRINTS
Picture page 62
Compote
Marigold £38/$70; Amethyst £48/$85

PANSY . . .

AUSTRALIAN PANSY
Picture page 63
Dish – straight-edged
Marigold £165/$300

PANSY
Manufactured by USI   *Picture page 62*
Imperial Repro White Nappy
White £45/$45
with QUILT exterior

Early manufacture:
Bowl 8"+
Marigold £35/$65; Amethyst £125/$225; Green £68/$120;
Blue £200/$360
Creamer/Sugar
Marigold £15/$25; Amethyst £28/$50; Blue £28/$50;
Smoke £38/$70
Dresser Tray
Marigold £50/$90; Amethyst £70/$125; Green £70/$125;
Smoke £100/$180
Pickle Dish – oval
Marigold £28/$50; Amethyst £45/$80; Green £45/$80;
Blue £150/$270; Smoke £70/$125
Nappy (old only)
Marigold £28/$50; Green £48/$85
Plate – rare
Marigold £80/$145; Amethyst £200/$360;
Green £100/$180; Smoke £150/$270

PANTHER
Manufactured by USF   *Picture page 63*
Bowl – footed, 5"
Marigold £55/$55; Amethyst £225/$225;
Green £400/$400; Blue £225/$225; Pastel (Red) £1400/$1400;
White £350/$350
Bowl – footed, 10"
Marigold £95/$95; Amethyst £275/$275;
Green £800/$800; Blue £275/$275; White £780/$780

PARQUET (Ron May)
Manufactured in EUR   *Drawing by Ron May page 88*
Creamer
Marigold £28/$50

PARROTS & POMEGRANATES
Named in Australia
Bowl   *Drawing page 25*

PASTEL SWAN
see SWAN . . .PASTEL SWAN
Manufactured by USD, USF, USN

PEACH

PEACH
Manufactured by USN
Bowl 5"
White £100/$100
Bowl 9"
White £200/$200
Sugar/Creamer
White £100/$100
Tumbler   *Picture page 79*
Blue £125/$125

PEACH & PEAR
Manufactured by USD   *Picture page 63*
Banana Bowl
Marigold £90/$90; Amethyst £145/$145

PEACOCK . . .

PEACOCK
Manufacturerd by USM

PEACOCK & DAHLIA
Manufactured by USF   *Picture page 63*
Bowl 7"+
Marigold £38/$38; Green £100/$100; Blue £100/$100;
Pastel (Ice Blue) £200/$200
Plate – 8", rare
Marigold £400/$400; Blue £500/$500

PEACOCK & GRAPE
Manufactured by USF   *Picture page 63*
Bowl – flat/footed
Marigold £45/$45; Amethyst £300/$300;
Green £200/$200; Blue £200/$200; Peach Opal £70/$70;
Amberina £1250/$1250
Plate – flat/footed, rare
Marigold £450/$450; Amethyst £350/$350;
Green £1000+/$1000; Blue £1500+/$1500; Pastel £400/$400
Bowl
Vaseline £680/$680

PEACOCK & URN
Manufactured by USF   *Picture page 63, 64*
Compote
Marigold on Aqua £250/$250
Bowl 8"+
Bearded Berry Exterior
Marigold on Milk Glass £3000+/$3000
Manufactured by USN
Ice Cream Bowl
Cobalt Blue £150/$150

PEACOCK AT THE FOUNTAIN
Manufactured by USN and USD   *Picture page 63, 82*
Tumbler
Marigold £75/$75; Amethyst £90/$90;
Green £90/$90; Blue £110/$110

PEACOCK ON THE FENCE
aka PEACOCKS
Manufactured by USN   *Picture page 64*
Bowl 8"+
Marigold £200/$200; Amethyst £325/$325;
Green £750/$750; Blue £750/$750;
Pastel (Ice Green) £1000+/$1000; White £/$ n/k
Plate 9"
Marigold £400/$400; Amethyst £600/$600;
Green £1000+/$1000; Blue £1000+/$1000;
Marigold on Aqua Opal £4000+/$4000

PEACOCK TAILS
Manufactured by USF   *Picture page 64*
Bon Bon
Marigold £55/$55; Amethyst £75/$75; Green £75/$75;
Blue £85/$85
Bowls 4"-10"
Marigold £40/$40; Amethyst £48/$48;
Green (rare) £240/$240; Blue £48/$48;
Peach Opal £500+/$500; Red £1500+/$1500
Compote
Marigold £40/$40; Amethyst £48/$48; Green £48/$48;
Blue £48/$48
Hat
Marigold £38/$38; Amethyst £45/$45; Green £45/$45;
Blue £45/$45
Plate 6"
Marigold £60/$60; Amethyst £70/$70
Plate 9"
Marigold £175/$175; Amethyst £200/$200;
Blue £150/$150

STRUTTING PEACOCK
Manufactured by Westmoreland USA   *Picture page 64*
Creamer or Sugar with lid
Amethyst £85/$85; Green £85/$85

PEBBLE & FAN
Manufactured by CZA   *Picture page 64*
Vase 11"+
Marigold £800/$1440; Blue £100/$1800;
Vaseline £1200/$2160

PERSIAN MEDALLIONS
Manufactured by USF   *Picture page 64*
Bon-Bon
Marigold £55/$55; Amethyst £75/$75; Green £85/$85;
Blue £95/$95; Red £100/$100; Aqua £200/$200
Compote
Marigold £85/$855; Green £165/$165; Blue £60/$60;
White £650/$650; Red £1100/$1100
Bowl 5", 8"
Marigold £45/$45; Amethyst £75/$75; Green £75/$75;
Blue £85/$85; Red £1100/$1100
Bowl 10"**
Marigold £65/$65; Amethyst £175/$175;
Green £265/$265; Blue £400+/$400
Orange Bowl
Marigold £65/$65; Amethyst £175/$175;
Green £2000+/$2000; Blue £175/$175
Rose Bowl
Marigold £45/$45; Amethyst £65/$65; Green £65/$65;
Blue £65/$65
Plate 7", 9"
Marigold £55/$55; Amethyst £200+/$200;
Green £500+/$500; Blue £175/$175
Punch Bowl – top and base
Marigold £220/$220; Amethyst £320/$320;
Green £360/$360; Blue £360/$360

PETALS & PRISMS (Derek White)
Drawing by Ron May page 88
Fruit Bowl
Marigold £28/$50

PETER RABBIT
Manufactured by USF   *Picture page 65*
Exterior pattern to PEACOCK & URN
Exterior pattern to LEAF CHAIN/ORANGE TREE
Bowl – rare
Marigold £800+/$800; Green £1200/$1200;
Blue £1200/$1200
Plate – 10"
Marigold £3600/$3600; Green £3750/$3750;
Blue £3600/$3600

PILLARS & FLUTE
Manufactured by USI
Often confused with *LUSTRE & CLEAR*
Compote
Marigold £30/$30
Rose Bowl
Marigold £30/$30
Creamer/Sugar
Marigold £25/$25
Celery Vase
Marigold £28/$28

PINCHED SWIRL
Manufactured by USD   *Picture page 65*
Vase with handworked top
Peach opalescent £100/$100

PINEAPPLE. . .

PINEAPPLE & BOWS
Manufactured by ESW
Sowerby UK
Bowl 4"
Marigold £28/$50; Amethyst £38/$70
Bowl 7"
Marigold £38/$70; Amethyst £58/$105
Creamer/Sugar
Marigold £28/$50; Amethyst £38/$70

Compote – stemmed
Marigold £48/$85; Amethyst £68/$120
Butter
Marigold £58/$105
Rose Bowl
Marigold £125/$225

PINEAPPLE CROWN (MQB)
Manufactured by FRI   *Picture page 78*
aka FOUR CROWNS
Plate
Marigold £165/$300

PINEAPPLE ROYAL
Manufactured by ENG   *Picture page 65*
Vase
Marigold £35/$65

PINECONE
Manufactured by USF   *Picture page 65*
See FIRCONE
Bowl 6"
Marigold £45/$45; Amethyst £65/$65

PIN-UPS
Named in Australia   *Picture page 65*
Bowl 8"+
Marigold £185/$335

PINWHEEL
Manufactured by ESW   *Picture page 65*
(part of the DERBY range NOT the USA (re Hartung)
PINWHEEL pattern)
Vase 6"+
Marigold £38/$70; Amethyst £85/$155
Vase 8"
Marigold £48/$85; Amethyst £125/$225
Bowl 8"

PLAID
Manufactured by Fenton USA   *Picture page 65*
Bowl 8"+
Green £300/$300; Blue £250/$250;
Pastel (Ice Blue) £1200/$1200
Plate 9"
Marigold £360/$360; Amethyst £400/$400

PLEATS (Ron May)
Manufactured by ESW   *Drawing by Ron May page 87*
Shallow Bowl/Plate
Marigold £18/$35

PODS & POSIES
See FLOWERS . . . FOUR FLOWERS

POINSETTIA
Manufactured by USN   *Picture page 65*
aka POINSETTIA & LATTICE
Bowl – flat or footed
Marigold £300/$300; Amethyst £465/$465;
Green £600/$600; Blue £800+/$800;
Aqua Opal £4000/$4000; Pastel (Ice Blue) £3000+/$3000

POND LILY
Manufactured by USF   *Picture page 65*
Bon Bon
on Clear £125/$125; Opaque Blue** £3000+

PONY
Manufactured by USD   *Picture page 66*
See also HORSES
Bowl 8"+ – internal or exterior
Marigold £80/$80; Amethyst £250/$250;
Marigold on Aqua £1250+/$1250

POPPY SHOW
Manufactured by USN　　　　　　*Picture page 66*
Plate 9"
Marigold £1500/$1500; Amethyst £1400/$1400;
Green £2000/$2000; Blue £2000/$2000;
Yellow base £3000/$3000

POWDER BOWL (BAMBI)
Manufactured in EUR　　　　　　*Picture page 66*
Marigold £65/$115

PREMIUM CANDLESTICK
Manufactured by USI　　　　　　*Picture page 80*
Marigold £85/$85 Each

PRISMA
Manufactured by SWE Lystercat circa 1925　　*Picture page 66*
Bowl
Marigold £85/$155; Blue £185/$335

PULLED LOOP
Manufactured by USD　　　　　　*Picture page 80*
Vase
Peach Opalescent £125/$125

PUMP
See TOWN PUMP

QUANDRY (MQB)
Manufactured by SWE　　　　　　*Picture page 66*
Bowl
Blue £165/$300

QUANTUM VASE (MQB)
Manufactured by SWE　　　　　　*Picture page 66*
Blue £365/$660

QUARTER BLOCK
Manufactured by ESW　　　　　　*Picture page 66*
Creamer/Sugar
Marigold £25/$45
Butter
Marigold £45/$80

QUATTRO
Named in Sweden (Source)　　　　*Picture page 66*
Bowl
Marigold £165/$300; Blue £265/$480

QUEENIE (MQB)
Manufactured by SWE　　　　　　*Picture page 66*
akin to QUANDRY but with a small pattern between panels
Bowl
Marigold £165/$300; Blue £265/$480

QUESTION MARKS
Manufactured by USD　　　　*Picture page 66, 81*
Compote – short stem
Marigold £38/$38; Amethyst £48/$48;
Peach Opal £68/$68
Cake Plate
Marigold £150/$150; Amethyst £425/$425;
Marigold £40/$40; Amethyst £65/$65;
Peach Opal £68/$68

QUILT
As exterior pattern to PANSY...
Nappy
Marigold £25/$45; Green £45/$80;
White – repro £45/$80

QUILT & STAR
Manufactured by FRI　　　　　　*Picture page 78*
Short Stubby Vase
Blue base £395/$710

QUILTED FANS (MQB)
Manufactured by FRI　　　　　　*Picture page 66*
Shallow Oblong Dish (Ext pattern only
Blue base £850/$1550

QUILTED PANELS (MQB)
Manufactured by FDK　　　　　　*Picture page 78*
Tumbler
Marigold £185/$335; Blue £285/$515

QUILTED ROSE (MQB)
Manufactured in Australia by SWE
See ROSE...QUILTED ROSE

QUINCE WATER JUG (MQB)
Manufactured by SWE　　　　　　*Picture page 66*
Marigold £85/$155

QUIVER (MQB)
Manufactured by SWE　　　　　　*Picture page 67*
Akin to QUANDRY & QUEENIE
Bowl
Marigold £165/$300; Blue £225/$405

RABBIT...
see PETER RABBIT

RANDEL
Manufactured by SWE (ex catalogue)
aka HAMBURG　　　*Drawing by John Masters page 38*

RANGER
aka BLOCKS & ARCHES

RAYS...

STIPPLED RAYS
Manufactured by USI　　　　　　*Picture page 73*
Creamer/Sugar
Marigold £30/$30; Green £45/$45
Manufactured by USN
Bowl 8", 10"+
Marigold £35/$35; Amethyst £48/$48; Green £58/$58
Compote
Marigold £48/$48; Amethyst £58/$58; Green £58/$58
Manufactured by USF
Bon Bon
Marigold £28/$28; Amethyst £38/$38; Green £38/$38;
Blue £48/$48
Bowl 5", 10"
Marigold £38/$38; Amethyst £48/$48; Green £48/$48;
Blue £48/$48
Compote
Marigold £28/$28; Amethyst £38/$38; Green £38/$38;
Blue £38/$38
Creamer/Sugar
Marigold £28/$28; Amethyst £38/$38; Green £38/$38;
Blue £38/$38

REX
Named in Sweden (Source)　　　　*Picture page 67*
Vase – turned top
Marigold £125/$225; Blue £225/$405; Milk Irid £1000/$1800
Vase – plain top
Marigold £85/$155; Blue £285/$515

RIBBON

RIBBON AND LEAVES
Manufactured by ENG　　　　　　*Picture page 67*
Marigold £38/$70

RIBBON SWAGS
Exterior pattern to WISHBONE　　　*Picture page 75*
Bowl on 3 legs
Amethust £125

- -

RIBBON SWIRL (MQB)
Manufactured by USI　　　*Picture page 67*
aka COLUMBIA (USA)
Giant Cake Plate on short stem
Marigold £150/$270

- -

RIBBON TIE
Manufactured by USF　　　*Picture page 67*
aka COMET
Bowl**
Marigold £160/$160; Amethyst £190/$190;
Green £200/$200; Blue £280/$280; Red £5000+/$5000
Plate 9"
Marigold £185/$185; Blue £285/$285

_____

RIIHIMAKI TUMBLER (MQB)
Manufactured by FRI named on base　　*Picture page 67, 78*
Tumbler – only one known
Blue £2880/$5185

_____

ROBIN
Manufactured by USI　　　*Picture page 81*
Tumbler
Marigold £60/$60

_____

ROCCOCO WAVES (Frank Horn)
Manufactured in USA　　　*Picture page 67*
Oil Lamp
See Opal Roccoco Waves

_____

ROSALIND
Manufactured by USM　　　*Picture page 67*
Bowl 5" – rare
Marigold £1200/$1200; Amethyst £250/$250;
Green £475/$475
Bowl 10"**
Marigold £225/$225; Amethyst £380/$380;
Green £265/$265; Pastel (Aqua) £400+/$400
Compote 8"
Marigold £100/$100

_____

ROSALIND WITH DIVING DOLPHIN FEET**
aka DOLPHINS
Picture page 67
Compote
Amethyst £650/$1170; Blue £500/$900

ROSE/ROSES . . .

BASKET OF ROSES
Named by Tom Sprain USA　　　*Picture page 68*
Bon Bon
Marigold £38/$38; Amethyst £60/$60
For stippled background add 100%

- -

CAPTIVE ROSE
Manufactured by USF　　　*Picture page 68*
Bon Bon
Marigold £45/$45; Amethyst £65/$65;
Green £65/$65; Blue £85/$85
Bowl 8"-10"
Marigold £75/$75; Amethyst £85/$85; Green £85/$85;
Blue £85/$85; Black Amethyst £250/$250
Compote
Marigold £45/$45; Amethyst £55/$55; Green £55/$55;
Blue £55/$55
Plate 7"
Marigold £100/$100; Amethyst £155/$155;
Green £175/$175; Blue £185/$185

Plate 10"
Marigold £185/$335; Amethyst £360/$650;
Green £380/$685; Blue £295/$530

- -

CIRCLED ROSE
Picture page 68
Bowl
Marigold on front with Australian Pansy and Cupid
£165/$300

- -

FINE CUT & ROSES
Manufactured by USN　　　*Picture page 68*
Rose Bowl – footed
Marigold £65/$65; Amethyst £125/$125;
Green £125/$125; Blue £125/$125
Candy Dish – footed
Marigold £65/$65; Amethyst £135/$135;
Green £140/$140; Blue £155/$155

- -

LARGE ROSE
Manufactured in EUR　　　*Picture page 80*
aka Rose Tumbler
Marigold £35/$65

- -

OPEN ROSE
Manufactured by USI　　　*Picture page 68*
Bowl – footed 9"
Marigold £40/$40; Amethyst £45/$45;
Green £45/$45
Fruit Bowl 7", 10"
Marigold £45/$45; Amethyst £55/$55;
Green £55/$55
Plate 9"
Marigold £45/$45; Amethyst £65/$65;
Green £65/$65
Rose Bowl
Marigold £28/$28; Amethyst £48/$48;
Green £48/$48

- -

QUILTED ROSE (MQB)
Picture page 68
Bowl with intaglio base pattern Rose
Marigold £65/$115

- -

ROSE & DIAMOND
USA name for ROSE GARDEN/ROSOR from Sweden

- -

ROSE PANELS
Possibly Scandinavian　　　*Picture page 68*
Compote – large
Marigold £125/$225

- -

ROSE SHOW
Manufactured by USN　　　*Picture page 68*
Bowl 8"+
Marigold £350/$350; Amethyst £650/$650;
Green £2500/$2500; Blue £1000/$1000;
Aqua Opal £1500+/$1500; Ice Blue £1800+/$1800
Plate
Marigold £1800/$1800; Amethyst £2000/$2000;
Green £7000/$7000; Blue £1200/$1200;
Aqua Opal £6000/$6000

- -

ROSE WREATH
Manufactured by USD　　　*Picture page 68*
Compote – large
Marigold £125/$125

- -

ROSOR
aka ROSE GARDEN or ROSE & DIAMOND
Picture page 68
Letter Vase – Large, extremely rare
Blue £1600/$2880

Letter Vase – small, 5"+
Blue £1200/$2160
Pitcher – large
Blue £950/$1710
Bowl
Has metal grid top when known as FLOWER BLOCK
Blue £65/$115
Banana Boat Bowl – extra large
Marigold £265/$480; Blue £365/$660

SERPENTINE ROSE
European   *Drawing by Ron May page 89*
Bowl – large, deep, footed
Marigold £65/$115

TEXAS ROSE
aka DOUBLE STEMMED ROSE
Manufactured by Dugan USA   *Picture page 69*
Bowl
Marigold £55/$100; Amethyst £65/$115;
Green £65/$115; Blue £75/$135;
Peach Opal £85/$155; Pastel (Celeste) £500+/$900

WILD ROSE
Manufactured by USN   *Picture page 69, 79*
Bowl – footed, open edge
Marigold £65/$65; Amethyst £75/$75;
Green £85/$85

WREATH OF ROSES
Manufactured by USF   *Picture page 69*
Punch Bowl set
*with Persan Medallions interior **
Marigold £2000+/$2000; Amethyst £275/$275;
Green £375/$375; Blue £400/$400; Peach Opal £2000/$2000
Punch Cup
Marigold £30/$30; Amethyst £38/$38; Green £38/$38;
Blue £45/$45

ROUND-UP
Manufactured by USD   *Picture page 69*
Same exterior as APPLE BLOSSOMS & FANCIFUL.
Interior to BIG BASKETWEAVE
Bowl 8"+ *
Marigold £60/$60; Amethyst £125/$125; Blue £200/$200;
Peach Opal £165/$165; White £120/$120
Plate 9"
Marigold £180/$180; Amethyst £220/$220;
Blue £400/$400; Peach Opal £300/$300; White £350/$350

ROWBOAT
Manufactured by Sowerby UK   *Picture page 69*
aka DAISY BLOCK ROWBOAT
Marigold £200/$360; Blue £260/$470; Aqua £300/$540

SAILBOATS
Manufactured by Fenton USA   *Picture page 69*
Bowl 6"
Marigold £38/$38; Green £75/$75; Blue £75/$75;
)Red £500/$500
Goblet
Marigold £200/$200; Amethyst £295/$295;
Green £225/$225; Blue £225/$225
Wine
Marigold £45/$45; Blue £100/$100
Compote
Marigold £65/$65; Blue £125/$125
Plate
Marigold £600+/$600; Blue £400+/$400

SALAD PANELS (MQB)
Manufactured by SWE   *Picture page 81*
Marigold £265/$480; Blue £365/$660

S-BAND
See BROKEN CHAIN

SCALE BAND
Manufactured by USF   *Picture page 69*
Bowl 6"
Marigold £30/$30; Peach Opal £75/$75;
White £80/$80
Plate 6"+
Marigold £45/$45; Red £500/$500
Plate – 7" plus domed base
Marigold £45/$45; Red £500/$500
Pitcher *
Marigold £125/$125; Peach Opal £350/$350
Tumbler
Marigold £60/$60; Peach Opal £300/$350

SCROLL & DAISY
Manufactured in Australia
Exterior pattern to KIWI

SCROLL EMBOSS
Manufactured by ESW   *Picture page 69*
Internal pattern to PINEAPPLE
Plate 7"
Manufactured by USI
Internal pattern to DIVING DOLPHINS and EASTERN STAR
Bowl 8"+
Marigold £45/$80; Amethyst £65/$115
Plate 9"
Marigold £180/$335; Amethyst £265/$480;
Green £210/$380
Compote – large & small
Marigold £40/$70
Sauce
Marigold £30/$55; Amethyst £40/$70

SEACOAST CUSPIDOR
Souvenir Spittoon   *Picture page 69*
Peach Opal £75/$135

SEAWEED . . .

SEAWEED
Manufactured by USM   *Picture page 69*
Bowl 5" – rare
Marigold £300/$300; Green £350/$350
Bowl 9"*
Marigold £200/$200; Green £300/$300; Blue £1200/$1200
Plate 10"
Marigold £800/$800; Amethyst £800/$800;
Green £860/$860
Ice Cream Bowl – 10"+
Marigold £300/$300; Amethyst £1200/$1200;
Green £880/$880

SEAWEED & CORAL (MQB)
Probably manufacted by CZA on Crackle
Only 1 known   *Picture page 69*
Vase 4 sided & enamelled
Marigold £1850/$3330

(FEATHERED) SERPENT
Manufactured by USF   *Picture page 70*
Bowl 5"
Marigold £35/$35; Amethyst £48/$48; Green £48/$48;
Blue £48/$48
Bowl 10"
Marigold £55/$55; Amethyst £95/$95; Green £95/$95;
Blue £95/$95
Spittoon
Amethyst £3500/$3500

SHELL . . .

BEADED SHELL
see BEADED SHELL Repro Mug

SHELL
Manufactured by USI   *Picture page 70*
Bowl 7", 9"
Marigold £35/$65; Amethyst £100/$180; Green £65/$115
Plate 8"+
Marigold £165/$300; Amethyst £1000+/$1800;
Green £285/$515

SHRIKE
Named in Australia   *Picture page 70*
aka THUNDERBIRD
Bowl – 5"
Marigold £125/$225; Black Amethyst £260/$470
Bowl – 9"
Marigold £280/$500; Black Amethyst £380/$685

SINGING BIRDS
Manufactured by USN
See also BIRDS. . . SINGING BIRDS

SIX PETALS
Manufactured by USD   *Picture page 70*
Bowl 8"+**
Marigold £40/$40; Amethyst £85/$85;
Green £85/$85; Blue £85/$85; Pastel £85/$85
Plate
Marigold £80/$80; Amethyst £120/$120;
Green £130/$130; Peach Opal £165/$165
Hat
Marigold £45/$45; Amethyst £65/$65; Green £65/$65

SMALL RIB
Manufactured by USD   *Picture page 70*
Compote
Marigold £65/$65; Amethyst £75/$75; Green £75/$75
Rose Bowl on stem
Marigold £65/$65; Amethyst £75/$75; Green £75/$75

SMOCKING (Lorna Payne)
See also POWDER BOWL (BAMBI)
Modern Indiana (USA)   *Picture page 70*
Powder Bowl and Lid
Blue £48/$85

SMOOTH RAYS PANELS
Manufactured by USI   *Picture page 70*
Plate – 8 sided
Smoke £125/$125

SNOW FANCY
Manufactured by McKee USA   *Picture page 70*
Bowl 5"
Marigold £50/$50
Creamer/Sugar – large
Marigold £65/$115

SODA GOLD
Manufactured by USI and FRI
Pitcher
Manufactured by FRI
"Rio" £165/$300
Tumbler
Marigold £28/$50

SOLDIERS & SAILORS
Manufactured by USF   *Picture page 70*
Commemorative Tray/Plate
Marigold £2000/$2000; Amethyst £1450/$1450;
Blue £2200/$2200

SOLROS (Source)
aka SUNFLOWER & DIAMONDS
See DIAMONDS . . .SOLROS

SONYA (MQB)
Manufactured by SWE   *Picture page 70*
Bowl
Marigold £185/$335 "Rio" base/Marigold irid £000/$000

SOPHIA (MQB)
Manufactured by SWE   *Picture page 70*
Vase on pedestal base
Marigold £125/$225; Pale brown base £195/$350

SPEARS & CHEVRONS (Ron May)
Drawing by Ron May page 88
Compote – small on stub legs
????Price

SPEARS & DIAMOND BANDS (Ron May)
Manufactured by ENG   *Drawing by Ron May page 89*
Vase
Marigold £30/$55

SPINNING STAR
See STAR . . . SPINNING STAR

SPIRIT OF '76
Manufactured in USA   *Picture page 71*
Commemorative Plate
Marigold £38/$38

SPITTOON

See SEACOST CUSPIDOR
See (FROCKLING) BEARS

SPRINGTIME
Manufactured by USN   *Picture page 71*
Butter
Marigold £300/$300; Amethyst £400/$400;
Green £420/$420
Sugar/Creamer
Marigold £300/$300; Amethyst £400/$400;
Green £420/$420
Pitcher **
Marigold £650/$650; Amethyst £880/$880;
Green £950/$950
Tumbler – rare
Marigold £80/$80; Amethyst £120/$120;
Green £200/$200; Pastel £300/$300

S-REPEAT
Manufactured by USD
Exterior pattern

STAG & HOLLY
Manufactured by USF   *Picture page 71*
Bowl 9", 13"
Marigold £100/$100; Amethyst £275/$275;
Green £680/$680; Blue £350/$350;
Peach Opal £1400/$1400; Red £2000/$2000
Rose Bowl – footed
Marigold £280/$280; Blue £850/$850
Plate – footed 9"
Marigold £880/$880; Amethyst £3000/$3000;
Blue £1600/$1600
Plate – footed 13"
Marigold £900/$900
Bowl – spat feet
Red £2000/$2000

STAR/STARS . . .

CURVED STAR
Manufactured by SWE   *Picture page 71*
Sugar – stemmed
Marigold £65 / $115; Blue £165 / $300
Creamer
Bowl – large
Marigold £65 / $115; Blue £200 / $360
Punch top plus base set
Marigold £265 / $480; Blue £365 / $660
Vase *(aka DAGNY/LASSE)*
Marigold £220 / $400; Blue £310 / $560
Chalice *(aka CATHEDRAL CHALICE)*
Marigold £125 / $225; Blue £265 / $480

DOUBLE STAR (MQB)
Manufactured by FDK   *Picture page 71*
Marigold £85 / $155; Blue £125 / $225

EASTERN STAR
Manufactured by SWE   *Picture page 71*
With SODA GOLD exterior pattern in USA (and possibly
Finland EDA STAR) (MQB)
Compote
Marigold £38 / $70

MANY STARS
Manufactured by USM   *Picture page 71*
Bowl**
Marigold £400 / $400; Amethyst £800 / $800;
Green £750 / $750; Blue £2200 / $2200

QUILT & STAR (MQB)
Manufactured by FRI   *Picture page 78*
Short Stubby Vase
Marigold £200 / $360; Blue £395 / $710

SPINNING STAR (MQB)
Manufactured by FDK   *Picture page 71*
Vase
Marigold £265 / $480; Blue £310 / $560

STAR & FAN (MQB)
Manufactured by SWE   *Picture page 72*
aka GLADER
Vase
Marigold £265 / $480; Blue £325 / $585

STAR & FILE
Manufactured by USI   *Picture page 72*
Decanter
Marigold £110 / $1100

STAR & HOBS (MQB)
Manufactured by SWE   *Picture page 72*
aka OREBRO (Sweden) and NORTHERN LIGHTS
Oval Bowl
Marigold £185 / $335; Blue £285 / $515
Banana Boat
Marigold £265 / $480; Blue £365 / $660

STAR & OVALS (MQB)
Manufactured by FRI   *Picture page 72*
Milk Jug
Marigold £28 / $50

STARS & PENDANTS (MQB)
Manufactured by EMK   *Picture page 72*
Compote on stem
Marigold £85 / $155

STAR & STUDS (MQB)
Manufactured by ESW   *Picture page 72*
Bowl on 3 legs
Marigold £48 / $85

STARBURST (MQB)
Manufactured by FRI   *Picture page 72*
Creamer/Sugar (each)
Blue £185 / $335

STARBURST & CROWN (MQB)
Manufactured by FRI   *Picture page 72, 79*
Tumbler
Marigold £165 / $300; Blue £265 / $480
Estonian Compote
Blue £365 / $660

STARBURST MEDALLIONS (MQB)
Manufactured by EMK   *Picture page 72*
Bowl
Blue £225 / $405

STARDUST (MQB)
Manufactured by EMK   *Picture page 72*
Bowl – small
Marigold £85 / $155

STARFISH
Manufactured by USD   *Picture page 81*
Compote
Peach Opal £150+ / $150

STARFLOWER
Manufactured by USF   *Picture page 72*
Pitcher**
Marigold £3000 / $3000; Peach Opal £1500 / $1500

STARLIGHT VASE
Manufactured by EMK   *Picture page 72*
Marigold £135 / $135

STAR OF DAVID
Manufactured by USI   *Picture page 72*
with ARCS exterior
Bowl
Marigold £70 / $70; Amethyst £250 / $250; Green £180 / $180

STAR OF DAVID & BOWS
Manufactured by USN   *Picture page 73*
Bowl 8"+
Marigold £60 / $110; Amethyst £150 / $270;
Green £100 / $180; Red £2500+ / $4500

STAR STRUCK (MQB)
Manufactured by SWE   *Picture page 73*
Bowl
Blue £365 / $660

STIPPLE & STAR (MQB)
Manufactured by FRI   *Picture page 78*
Vase
Marigold £225 / $405; Blue £365 / $660

STIPPLED RAYS & STARS (Ron May)
Manufactured in EUR   *Drawing by Ron May page 89*
Bowl – small, deep
Marigold £28 / $50

STJARNA (Source)
Manufactured by SWE   *Picture page 73*
Bonbonniere
Blue £1500 / $2700

VERTICAL STAR PANELS (MQB)   *Picture page 73*
Manufactured by FDK
Bonbonniere and Lid
Blue £1000/$1800

- -

WHIRLING STAR
Manufactured in Europe and by USI   *Picture page 81*
Punch Cup
Marigold £30/$30

STIPPLED RAYS
Manufactured by USF   *Picture page 73*
Bowl – 10", squared off
Blue £465/$465

STORK & RUSHES
Manufactured by USD   *Picture page 73, 78*
See SUMMERS DAY VASE
Punch Bowl top and vase base
Marigold £125/$125; Amethyst £220/$220; Blue £240/$240
Hat
Marigold £28/$28; Amethyst £55/$55; Blue £55/$55
Pitcher
Marigold £200/$200; Amethyst £220/$220; Blue £400/$400
Tumbler
Marigold £38/$38; Amethyst £38/$38; Blue £48/$48

STRAWBERRY . . .

(INTAGLIO) STRAWBERRY
Picture page 79
Souvenir 88 Mug – Modern
Blue £58/$105; Vaseline opalescent £58/$105

- -

STRAWBERRY
Manufactured by USF   *Picture page 73*
Bon-Bon
Marigold £45/$45; Amethyst £50/$50; Green £50/$50;
Blue £100/$100
Manufactured by USM
Bowl 6"+
Marigold £65/$65; Amethyst £100/$100; Green £90/$90
Bowl 8", 10" – scarce
Marigod £210/$210; Amethyst £375/$375; Green £375/$375
Compote – rare
Marigold £430/$430; Amethyst £375/$375; Green £375/$375
Banana Boat – extremely rare
Manufactured by USN
Bowl 5"
Marigold £35/$35; Amethyst £45/$45; Green £45/$45;
Blue £55/$55
Bowl 10"
Marigold £105/$105; Amethyst £310/$310;
Green £225/$225; Blue £310/$310; Pastel £1000+/$1000;
Aqua Opal £2000+/$2000
Plate 9"
Marigold £225/$225; Amethyst £380/$380;
Green £310/$310; Blue £310/$310;
Aqua Opal £2500+/$2500
Plate – handgrip edge
Marigold £160/$160; Amethyst £175/$175;
Green £175/$175; Blue £180/$180

- -

STRAWBERRY SCROLL
Manufactured by USF   *Picture page 73*
Pitcher
Marigold £3750/$3750; Blue £3200/$3200
Tumbler**
Marigold £250/$250; Blue £280/$280

- -

WILD STRAWBERRY
Manufactured by USN   *Picture page 73*
Bowl – large
Marigold £165/$165; Amethyst £260/$260;
Green £260/$260; Peach Opal £300+/$300
Bowl – small 6"
Marigold £60/$60; Amethyst £120/$120; Blue £140/$140
Side upturned add 25%
Plate (*a larger variation on STRAWBERRY*)
Marigold £165/$165; Amethyst £325/$325

STRETCH TUMBLER
Picture page 80
Marigold £35/$65

SUMMERS DAY VASE
Base to Stork & Rushes Punch Bowl set   *Picture page 73*
Marigold £80/$145

SUNFLOWER . . .

SUNFLOWER
Manufactured by USN   *Picture page 73*
With MEANDER exterior pattern
Bowl 8"+
Marigold £45/$45; Amethyst £65/$65; Green £65/$65
Plate
Marigold £200/$200; Green £400/$400

- -

SUNFLOWER & DIAMONDS
Manufactured by SWE   *Picture page 83*
aka SOLROS
Vases – two
Marigold £165/$300; Green £380/$685; Blue £380/$685

SUNGOLD
Origin unknown   *Picture page 74*
*Pattern as SUNGOLD (**Hartung**). Different from the*
*SUNGOLD EPERGNE (**Bill Edwards**)*
Plate
Marigold £125/$225

SUNGOLD FLORAL (MQB)
Manufacturer not known   *Picture page 74*
Bowl
Marigold £85/$155

SUNSPRAY EPERGNE (MQB)
Origin unknown   *Picture page 74*
This has SUNGOLD base plate as per M.Hartung.
Marigold £265/$480

SVEA (Source)
Named in Sweden Eda   *Picture page 74*
Bowl
Marigold £38/$70; Blue £68/$120
Vase
Marigold £58/$105
Pickle
Marigold £48/$85
Pin Tray
Marigold £28/$50; Blue £48/$85

SWAN . . .

AUSTRALIAN SWAN   *Picture page 74*
Bowl
Black Amethyst £235/$425

- -

COVERED SWAN BUTTER
Manufactured by ESW
See COVERED SWAN

NESTING SWAN
Manufactured by USM   *Picture page 74*
DIAMOND & FAN exterior
Bowl – 9"
Marigold £200/$200; Amethyst £300/$300;
Green £400/$400; Blue £2000+/$2000

SWAN & CATTAILS
Picture page 79
Toothpick Holder repro
Blue £48/$85

SWATHE & DIAMOND*
Manufactured in ENG   *Picture page 74*
aka STIPPLED DIAMOND SWAG
Compote
Marigold £28/$50; Amethyst £38/$70

SWEDISH CROWN (MQB)
Manufactured SWE   *Picture page 74*
Bowl
Blue £325/$585

SWIRLED HOBNAIL
See HOBNAIL . . . SWIRLED HOBNAIL

TEN MUMS
Manufactured by USF   *Picture page 74*
Bowl – 8"
Marigold £65/$65; Amethyst £95/$95; Green £160/$160;
Blue £285/$285
Bowl – 9" footed, rare
Marigold £450/$450
Plate 10"
Blue £800+/$800
Pitcher
Marigold £500/$500; Blue £800+/$800
Tumbler – rare
Marigold £70/$70; Blue £120/$120; White £300/$300

TEXAS ROSE
aka DOUBLE STEMMED ROSE
See ROSE . . . TEXAS ROSE

THISTLE . . .

GOLDEN THISTLE
Manufacturer not known   *Picture page 75*
Pin Tray – 5"
On "Rio"(Pink) Base glass £260+/$470

THISTLE
Manufactured by USF   *Picture page 75*
Banana Boat
Marigold £300/$300; Amethyst £400/$400;
Green £500/$500; Blue £550/$550

THISTLE BOWL
Manufactured by USF   *Picture page 74*
Marigold £80/$80; Amethyst £120/$120;
Green £140/$140; Blue £130/$130

THISTLE VASE
Manufactured in EUR   *Picture page 75*
Marigold £28/$50

THUNDERBIRD
Manufactured in Australia
See alternative name SHRIKE

TIGER LILY
Manufactured by USI   *Picture page 75, 78*
Tumbler
Marigold £35/$35
Manufactured by FRI

Pitcher
Blue £420/$755
Manufactured by EMK
Tumbler
Marigold £85/$155

TOFFEE BLOCK
Picture page 75
Pitcher
Marigold £28/$50

TOKYO (MQB)
Manufactured by SWE (ex catalogue)   *Picture page 75*
aka TOKIO
Bowl – deep
Marigold £950/$1710; Blue £1850/$3330

TOOTHPICK HOLDERS
See AFRICAN SHIELD
See SWAN & CATTAILS

TOOLS
From Eda Sweden   *Picture page 79*

TOWN PUMP
Repro award   *Picture page 81*
Purple £58/$105

TREE TRUNK VASE
Manufactured by USN   *Picture page 75*
Marigold £225/$225; Amethyst £185/$185;
Green £205/$205; Blue £325/$325; Aqua Opal £1200/$1200

TRIO
Manufactured by SWE (ex catalogue)   *Picture page 75*
Bowl
Marigold £200/$360; Blue £300/$540

TROUT & FLY
Manufactured by USM   *Picture page 75*
See also FISH
Bowl**
Marigold £650/$650; Amethyst £600/$600;
Green £880/$880

TULIP . . .

BUTTERFLY & TULIP
See BUTTERFLY . . . BUTTERFLY & TULIP

REGAL TULIP (Lorna Payne)
Possibly Dutch   *Picture page 76*
Vase
Marigold £68/$120

TULIP & CORD (MQB)
Manufactured by FRI   *Picture page 75*
Mug
Marigold £650/$1170

TURKU (Source)
Manufactured by FRI   *Picture page 76*
Commemorative Ash Tray
Marigold £365/$660

TWIN LILIES
See WINDFLOWER . . . TWIN LILIES

TWINS
Manufactured by USI   *Picture page 76*
Bowl – 5"
Marigold £20/$20; Green £35/$35
Bowl – 9"
Marigold £25/$25; Green £45/$45

TWO EYED ELK
See ELK . . . ATLANTIC CITY ELK

UNA (MQB)
Manufactured by SWE (ex catalogue)   *Picture page 76*
Bowl – deep
Marigold £165/$300

VERA VASE (MQB)
Manufactured by SWE   *Picture page 76*
On pedestal base
Blue £410/$740

VERTICAL STAR PANELSS
See STAR . . . VERTICAL STAR PANELS

VINING LEAF . . .

VINING LEAF PERFUME
Possibly Dutch or Czechoslovakian   *Picture page 76*
Perfume Bottle and Stopper
Marigold on clear £85/$155

VINING LEAF VASE
NB. There is a Variant which has small leaves to the pattern
Marigold £65/$115

VINLOV (Source)
Manufactured by SWE (ex catalogue)   *Picture on page 76*
Banana Boat
Amethyst £1850/$3330

VINTAGE . . .

VINTAGE
Manufactured by USM **Bowl 5"**
Marigold £650/$650; Green £850/$850; Blue £1650/$1650
Bowl 9"
Marigold £480/$850; Amethyst £760/$1370;
Green £680/$680; Blue £3000/$3000
Manufactured by US
Perfume & Stopper
Marigold £295/$295; Amethyst £485/$485
Powder Bowl
Marigold £50/$50; Amethyst £85/$85; Blue £95/$95
Manufactured by USF   *Picture page 76, 80*
Bowls 4"
Marigold £30/$30; Amethyst £38/$38; Green £38/$38;
Blue £38/$38
Compote
Marigold £38/$38; Amethyst £48/$48; Green £48/$48;
Blue £48/$48
Fernery – 9" bowl
Marigold £45/$45; Amethyst £55/$55; Green £65/$65;
Blue £65/$65
Epergne
Marigold £85/$85; Amethyst £110/$110; Green £125/$125;
Blue £125/$125
Plate 7"+
Marigold £280/$280; Amethyst £420/$420;
Green £220/$220; Blue £95/$95
Plate 11"
Marigold £175/$175; Green £210/$210; Blue £220/$220
Punch Bowl set
Marigold £225/$225; Amethyst £310/$310;
Green £365/$365; Blue £385/$385
Punch Cup
Marigold £28/$28; Amethyst £38/$38; Green £38/$38;
Blue £38/$38
Rose Bowl
Marigold £45/$45; Blue £35/$35
Spittoon
Marigold £6000+/$6000

Bowl – 8"
Red £3000/$5400

VINTAGE BANDED
Manufactured by USD   *Picture page 80*
Tumbler
Green (rare) £600

VINTAGE LEAF
Manufactured by USF   *Picture page 76*
See GRAPE . . . VINTAGE for variants
Bowl
Marigold £45/$45; Amethyst £65/$65; Green £65/$65;
Blue £65/$65

WAFFLE BLOCK
Manufactured by USI   *Picture page 76, 82*
Basket – 10"
Marigold £75/$75
Bowl
Marigold £38/$38
Creamer/Sugar
Marigold £28/$28
Vase
Marigold £38/$38
Pitcher
Marigold £120/$120
Tumbler
Marigold £200/$200
Rose Bowl
Marigold £65/$65
Punch Base & top
Marigold £185/$185
Punch Cup
Marigold £28/$50

WARRIOR
See similar pattern: STAR . . . SHOOTING STAR

WATERLILY

WATERLILY
Manufactured by USF   *Picture page 76*
Bowl – footed 6"
Marigold £40/$40; Amethyst £55/$55; Green £250/$250;
Blue £100/$100; Marbled base £125/$125
Bowl – footed 10"
Marigold £125/$125; Amethyst £95/$95;
Green £320/$320; Blue £180/$180

WATERLILY AND CATTAILS
Manufactured by USF   *Picture page 76*
Banana Boat
Blue £265/$265
Bon Bon
Marigold £45/$45; Amethyst £70/$70; Blue £80/$80
Pitcher
Marigold £300/$300; Blue £5000+/$5000
Tumbler
Marigold £80/$80
As exterior pattern to THISTLE BOWL

WATERLILY & DRAGONFLY**
Named in Australia   *Picture page 76*
Shallow 10" wide bowl
Marigold £160/$290

WHIRLING LEAVES
Manufactured by USM   *Picture page 77*
Internal pattern to FINE CUT OVALS
Bowl 9", 11"*
Marigold £75/$75; Amethyst £180/$180;
Green £220/$220

117

WHITE PITCHER**
Manufactured by USF   *Picture page 77*
£ n/k $ n/k

WICKERWORK
Manufactured by ESW and SWE   *Picture page 77*
Tripod Base and upturned edge plate
Marigold £225/$405; Amethyst £365/$660
Plate flat
Marigold £120/$215
Upturned edge plate
Marigold £135/$245

WIDE PANELS
Manufactured by USF & and USI   *Picture page 77*
Punch Bowl Top
As exterior pattern to HEAVY GRAPE
Amethyst £350/$350
Also found as exterior pattern to BLACKBERRY WREATH

WILD BLACKBERRY
Manufactured by USF
See BLACKBERRY. . .

WILD ROSE
see ROSE. . .WILD ROSE

WILLS GOLD FLAKE ASH TRAY
Manufactured by ENG   *Picture page 77*
Marigold (rare) £125/$225

WINDFLOWER
Manufactured by USD   *Picture page 77*
aka TWIN LILIES
Bowl 8"+
Marigold £38/$38; Blue £58/$58
Plate 9"+
Marigold £125/$125; Blue £210/$210
Nappy
Marigold £65/$65; Amethyst £75/$75; Blue £135/$135

WINDMILL
Manufactured by USI   *Picture page 77, 80*
Bowl 5"
Marigold £18/$18; Amethyst £25/$25; Green £25/$25
Bowl 9"
Marigold £30/$30; Amethyst £58/$58; Green £58/$58
Fruit Bowl 10"+
Marigold £40/$40; Green £40/$40
Pickle Dish
Marigold £28/$28; Green £38/$38
Water Jug/Milk
Marigold £48/$48; Amethyst £120/$120; Blue £80/$80;
Pastel £110/$110
Pitcher
Marigold £125/$125; Amethyst £300/$300;
Green £95/$95; Pastel £425/$425
Tumbler
Marigold £28/$28; Amethyst £175/$175; Green £38/$38
variant DOUBLE DUTCH
Bowl
Clambroth £110/$110

WISHBONE
Manufactured by USN   *Picture page 77*
See also RIBBON SWAGS as exterior pattern
Bowl 8", 10"
Marigold £75/$75; Amethyst £100/$100; Green £100/$100;
Blue £110/$110; Peach Opal £160/$160
Bowl footed
Marigold £125/$125; Amethyst £125/$125;
Green £125/$125

Epergne
Marigold £400/$720; Amethyst £1500+/$2700;
Green £2000/$3600
Plate – flat, rare
Marigold £2000/$3600; Amethyst £600+/$1080;
Plate – footed, rare
Marigold £2750/$4950; Amethyst £1750+/$3150;
Green £4000/$7200
Pitcher – rare
Marigold £750/$1350; Amethyst £750/$1350;
Green £850/$1550
Tumbler
Marigold £100/$180; Amethyst £138/$250;
Green £138/2500; Blue £150/$270; Peach Opal £200/$360

WREATHED CHERRY
See CHERRY . . . WREATHED CHERRY

WREATH OF ROSES
see ROSES . . . WREATH OF ROSES

YORK (Source)
Manufactured by SWE (ex catalogue)   *Picture page 77*
Bowl – deep, large
Marigold £165/$300; Blue £265/$480
Vase
Marigold £165/$300; Blue £265/$480

ZEPHYR DECANTER (MQB)
Origin unknown   *Picture page 78*
Marigold £65/$115

ZERO VASE (MQB)   *Picture page 78*
Marigold £48/$85

ZIG-ZAG
Manufactured by USM
Bowl
Marigold £220/$220; Amethyst £360/$360;
Green £295/$295
Bowl Tri-cornered** – 10"
Marigold £380/$380; Amethyst £465/$465;
Green £465/$465

ZILLERTAL (MQB)
Modern Austrian iridised beer bottle   *Picture page 82*
Amber base £38/$70

ZINNIA (MQB)
Origin unknown   *Picture page 78*
Decanter
Marigold £55/$100

ZIPPER ROUND (Ron May)
Manufactured in EUR   *Drawing by Ron May page 89*
aka CHECKERBOARD PANELS (USA) and ZIP-A-ROUND
Bowl, large, shallow
Marigold £58/$105

A List of Standard Colour Shadings in Carnival Glass

M= Marigold
A= Amethyst
G= Green
B= Blue

PO= Peach Opalescent
AO= Aqua Oplaescent
PAS= Pastels
R/J = Red or Jet

A List of Rarer Shadings

Amber
Amberina
Alaskan Green
Amethyst
Amethyst Opalescent
 Apricot
Aqua
Aqua Opalescent
Black Amethyst
Blue
Blue Opalescent
Celeste Blue B
Champagne
Citrene
Clambroth
Clear
Cranberry
Electric Blue
Emerald Green
Horehound
Ice Blue
Ice Green
Iridised Chocolate
Iridised Crackle
Iridised Custard
Iridised Milkglass
Iridised Moonstone
Iridised Slag
Iridised Stretch

Lavender
Lime Green
Lime Opalescent
Marigold
Marigold Custard
Marigold Milk Glass
Marigold Opalescent
Milkglass Opalescent
Nile Green
Pastel Marigold
Peach Opalescent
Pearl Opalescent
Persian Blue
Pink
Renniger Blue
Reverse Amberina
Russet Green
Sapphire
Smoke
Smoke Milkglass
Teal
Vaseline
Vaseline Opalescent
White
White Opalescent =
Wisteria
Yellow

About the contributors

Author: Marion Quintin-Baxendale B.A.(Hons), TEFL Cert.
Born Bath, Somerset, educated: City Bath Girls' Grammar School, Buckingham University (BA Hons European Studies), London University TEFL Certificate.

Extensively travelled worldwide, and has lived for several years each in France, Italy, Singapore, and Malta. Fluent in French and Italian. Studying Spanish and Rumanian. Interests: Travel. Languages, Poetry, Genealogy ,Antiques, Yoga, Gardening, Cooking. Author of *Carnival Glass Worldwide* in 1983. Published poet and recipient of several awards for poetry with International Society of Poets. Currently working on two volumes of Poetry for publication.

A collector of Carnival Glass, as well as other antiques, for over 30 years. Interested in the history of artefacts as well as in their aesthetic and artistic appeal. Has travelled to Scandinavia, Australia and America for Carnival Glass studies and researched at major production sources worldwide.

Principal Photographer: Gunnar Lersjo of Sweden
Former Secondary School Headmaster. Field: Economic History and Art, now retired. An established historical researcher and author producing books and Exhibitions on early local photographers and their work. Since 1977 has had four books on glass history published in Sweden. And from the 1960's has specialised as a Glass Photographer. Photography in this book was voluntarily provided.

Principal Artist: Ron May
Enjoyed a creative career as a Visualiser in Advertising and later, as a journalist and Commercial artist in publishing for over 40 years. Now retired, formerly held positions of Art Editor and Studio Manager within the National Magazine Company, the International Publishing Company and the Thomson Group Publications company. A keen collector of Carnival Glass and previous Vice President of the early Carnival Club of Great Britain. Drawings in this book were voluntarily provided.

Fenton Museum Glass: Photography
Permission to photograph kindly given by Frank Fenton of Fenton Art Glass Co. Photography undertaken, voluntarily, by Mr Howard Seufer of West Virginia, former Quality Control Manager at Fenton Art Glass Co and an avid amateur photographer.

Acknowledgements
Personal and professional

Personal acknowledgements to:
Mr Gunnar Lersjo of Arvika Sweden, Glass Historian and Principal Photographer of the majority of the glass in this book and without whose assistance this work would never have appeared. His assistance carried out on a purely voluntary basis and entailing many, many hours of dedicated research as well as photography. Where photographed by other sources, then so noted. See page 00.
Mr and Mrs Shirley Horn of Frank and Shirley Fairs and Auctions of UK, who kindly lent their assistance to the compiling of the Price List in this book and who freely presented much glass for photography as well.
Mr Frank Fenton of Fenton Art Glass USA for his personal and professional assistance in making much information available to me on a visit to the Fenton Factory, and to all his staff.
Mr Howard Seufer (USA) who voluntarily offered to photograph the Fenton Museum pieces that appear in this book. And at very short notice too!
Mr Ron May, of Hadleigh Essex UK, Principal Artist for this book, who produced his drawings on a purely voluntary basis. These generously and freely offered from his extensive collection of Carnival Glass drawings, the result of many years of study concerning this ware.
Mr and Mrs Ian Payne for assistance in pattern identification.
Mr Alan Woodgate for offering glass for photography.
For my family – Polly, Julia and Iram, Alexander and Helen, And to my special friends Cindy and Mick, Jo and Dave, Lorna and family, Lynn and Gary, Mary Jo and Bob, Pat, Ruth and Trevor, and Sylvia in Italy for their invaluable encouragement.
And last, but not least, to all those friends and collectors too numerous to name individually (but who know who they are!) who assisted me so ably in tracking down glass facts and figures, for this work.

Professional acknowledgements (in alphabetical order of country)
 These appertain to research over a long period of years, both for this book and for the earlier Carnival Glass Worldwide.
Australia
A.C.I. Australian Glass Manufacturers Co, Sydney, and the Community Services Manager Mr P K Harris.
Australian Carnival Enthusiasts Club for kind permission to refer to drawings and articles in the club newsletters
Australian Glass Workers Union, Sydney Australia and earlier Secretary Mr Jim Gibson
Mr Jack Burchmore of Bexley, N.S.W. for technical information
Mrs Pat Cubeta and Mrs M Dickinson for kind assistance
Mrs Marjorie Graham for kind permission to quote from her book Australian Glass of the Nineteenth and early Twentieth Century (see Bibliography)
Mr G Kirby of Canberra for practical assistance
Mr Eric Lockwood and the late Mr G Pomeroy for invaluable help with slides
Members of the Plate Sheet And Ornamental Glassworkers Union, Sydney
Mrs Triplett and the late Mr Triplett for kind assistance with slides.
Czechoslovakia
Bohemia Glassexport Co Ltd of England and Dr F Vacek
Museum of Arts and Industry and past and present Curators
Denmark
Holmegaards Glasvaerkers, Copenhagen and workers

England

Mr M V Arnold who kindly arranged contact with Australian collectors for slides used in this book

Mr R J Barry for provision of slide

Mrs Freck-Hagendorf for free translation of a difficult and technical German text

Mr Ron May, Principal (and voluntary) artist for the pattern drawings in this book

Shipley Art Gallery, Gateshead and Curator for permission to reprint a photograph of a Sowerby mould, through the Tyne and Wear County Museums.

Mrs M Spurrell for ink drawings

Mr John Watson for pencil drawings

Estonia

Tallinna Museum, Tallinn Estonia: Director M Varrak and Keeper of Glass Urve Mankin

Glass Artist Maare Saare of Tallinn Estonia

Tartu City Museum Tartu Estonia: especially to Mrs Pullerits.

Voru Museum and staff, Voru, Estonia

Rakvere Museum Rakvere Estonia: Director Olave Mae

Estonia History Museum, Estonia: Director Toomas Tamla also to Rein Laur, Aino Lepp, Maie Raun, Aita Raik

and Mau Parmas for photographs of their glass.

Finland

A. Ahlstrom Osakeyhtio of Karhula and Mr Eero Kojonen who provided details of a spectographic analysis of Karhula Lustre Ware

Karhula Lasimuseo and Curators past and present, particularly Mrs Inkeri Nyholm

Iittala Lasimuseo and Curators, especially Ms Marketa Kiemola

Suomen Lasimuseo, Riihimaki and Curators past and present, particularly Mrs Kaisa Koivisto

Mr Erkki Vaalle of Riihimaki for professional photography

Wartsila-Nuutajarvi Glass and early PR Manager Mrs Marjut Kumela

France and Belgium

Baccarat, S.A., NE France

Compagnie des Cristalleries de St Louis, Lemberg

Musée du Verre, Liege, Belgium. and Curators past and present.

Dr Giuseppe Cappa of Luxembourg

Musée du Verre 'art et technique', Charleroi N France

and to M. Claude Boland.

Germany

Bundesverband der Glasindustrie, Dusseldorf

Kungstggewerbe Museum, Berlin and Curators, especially Dr Walter Neuwirth.

Osterreichisches Museum fur angewandte Kunst, especially to Dr Waltrand Neuwirth

Holland

Museum Bergmans-var-Benningen, Rotterdam, and Curators, especially Ms Doris Kukyen-Schneider and Mr A Copier previous Chief Designer for Royal Leerdam Glassworks.

Royal Leerdam Glass and the late Mr Floris Meydam a previous Chief Designer for Royal Leerdam.

Mrs M J H Singelenburg-Van der Mer of Utrecht.

Mr W F Tonnekreek, Heideland

Norway

Magnor Glassworks, for permission to photograph moulds and glassmaking from its stores and Museum Shop.

Kunstindustrimuseet, Oslo and Curators, especially Ms Inger-Marie Lie.

Sweden

All those collectors who allowed pieces from Eda to be photographed for this book, especially the following:

Mr David Bergman for permission to use slides of Eda ware from his own collection.

Mr Gunnar Lersjo Glass Historian and Author who voluntarily undertook to photograph the majority of glass that appears in this Collectors' Guide. as well as researching the EDA records for requested information.

Swedish Workers Educational Authority (ABF Vastra Varmlands), who provided, free of charge and with the help of Mr G Lersjo, much detailed research information and photographic material relating to Eda Glassworks

Nordiska Museet, Stockhom and Curators, especially Mrs Inger Bonge-Bergrengren.

Stiftelsen Smalands Museum and Curators, especially Mr Lars Thor.

Varmlands Museum, Karlstad and Curators, especially Ms Helene Sjunneson.

United States of America

Fenton Art Glass Company of Williamstown Ohio and to Mr Frank Fenton personally and to *all* the staff for wonderful hospitality and invaluable assistance with regards to Fenton Carnival Glass production.

Particular thanks to Bob Hill, Supervisor of the Mould Shops, and to Tom Meiser and Alan Van Dyke, skilled mould Makers at Fenton Art Glass Company.

Also for kind permission to photograph many rare pieces from the Fenton Glass Museum, with the voluntary aid of Photographer Mr Howard Seufer.

Bibliography

Glass John A Brooks, Sampson Low Collectors Library
Imperial Carnival Glass Carl O Burns, Collector Books USA, 1996
The Early Victorian Period 1830-1860 The Connoisseur Period Guides, London.
Carnival Glass Standard Encyclopedia Bill Edwards,1995
Rarities in Carnival Glass" Bill Edwards, Collector Books USA, 1978
English Table Glass E. M. Elville, London Country Life Ltd
Australian Glass of the Nineteenth century and early Twentieth Century Marjorie Graham, David Ell Press, Sydney, Australia
Carnival in Lights Helen D Greguire, USA 1975
British Glass 1800-1914 Charles Hajdamach, Antique Collectors' Club 1991
Carnival Glass and *Carnival Club of Great Britain* Angela Hallam, articles.
Colors in Carnival Glass Sherman Hand, 1-1V USA 1972
The Collectors Encyclopedia of Carnival Glass Sherman Hand, 1-1V USA 1978
Carnival Glass Pattern Books 1-10 Marion Hartung, 1964-73
Glass through the age E.B. Haynes, Penguin, Harmondsworth, 1959
Encyclopedia of Victorian Coloured Glass William Heacock, various volumes, Peacock Publications, Columbus Ohio USA
The Glass Collector, and *Dugan/Diamond* William Heacock, James Measell & Berry Wiggins, Antique Publications, USA.
Glass W. B. Honey, Victoria and Albert Museum Publications, London
The Collector's Guide to Carnival Glass Marion Klamkin, USA 1976
Eda Glasbruk Lersjo and Fogelberg, Karlstad, Sweden 1977
The Shape of Things in Carnival Glass Donald E Moore, USA 1975
Victorian Table Glass & Ornaments Barbara Morris, London 1978
Carnival Glass Tumblesr Richard E Owens, USA 1973
Curiosities of Glassmaking A PELLATT, London 1849
Le Val-Saint-Lambert, ses Cristalleries et l'art du verre en Belgique Joseph Philippe, Liege. Edition Eugene Wahle, 1980
Glass- its traditions and its makers Ada Polak, G P Putnam, N York 1975
Pottery Gazettes London Victoria and Albert Museum
Glassmaking in England H, J. Powell, Cambridge University Press 1923
Carnival & Iridescent Glass Rose M Presznick, 4 vols 1964-67
Nineteenth Century Glass: its Genesis & Development Albert Christian Revi, USA 1967
American and European Pressed Glass in the Corning Museum of Glass Jane Shadel Spillman, USA 1981
Die Glasmakerei und Glasatzerei insbesonders nach ihrer chemischen Grundlagen L Springer, Zwiesel 1923
Pressing Glass Roy E Swaine. Glass Industry 1930 Vol 11, pp 204, Journal of the Society of Glass Technology 1930 vol 14, abs 368
English Glass W A. Thorpe, A. & C Black 1949
Le Verre Geoffrey Wills, Grange Bateliere, Paris 1973

NOTES

NOTES

PRICE GUIDE UPDATE

From March 1999 we will be producing an update of the price guide shown in this book, with more additions in terms of patterns and colours, and of course, prices as they have changed.

Please call us for this – telephone 0181 318 9580.

The price is just £3.00

Overseas – orders by credit card only!
UK – send cheque or pay by credit card.

Also if you have any rare or unusual items not listed in this book we would like to know about them. Photographs would be greatly appreciated, but we regret we cannot return them.

Call us on 0181 318 9580 for your update

Francis Joseph
5 Southbrook Mews
London SE12 8LG
Telephone: 0181 318 9580
Fax: 0181 318 1985

The Carnival Glass Society (UK)
P O Box 14, Hayes, Middlesex, UB3 5NU England

For a modest subscription, membership of the Carnival Glass Society (UK) offers you the following benefits:

The Carnival Glass Society
Newsletter 83   February 98

THIS ISSUE:-

The First in a series on
Australian Carnival Glass
from Gary Workman

Alphonse Tvaryanas on
Smoke and another
Millersburg misattribution

Richard Sinclair on Plates

Alan Sedgwick on the Folk Art
influences in CG Patterns

The Beginners' Page starts

◆ **Annual Convention** featuring the AGM, lecture, carnival glass sale, dinner, outings and visits.

◆ Regular **Newsletter** containing light and serious articles on glass and club activities, research features, both colour and black and white pictures.

◆ Local membership **get-togethers** with the opportunity to exchange views and Carnival Glass.

The Society welcomes members from both home and abroad. The Society's objectives are to give collectors the opportunity to meet, to exchange views and information, and to publish accurate details about manufactures, patterns, shapes and colours of Carnival Glass.